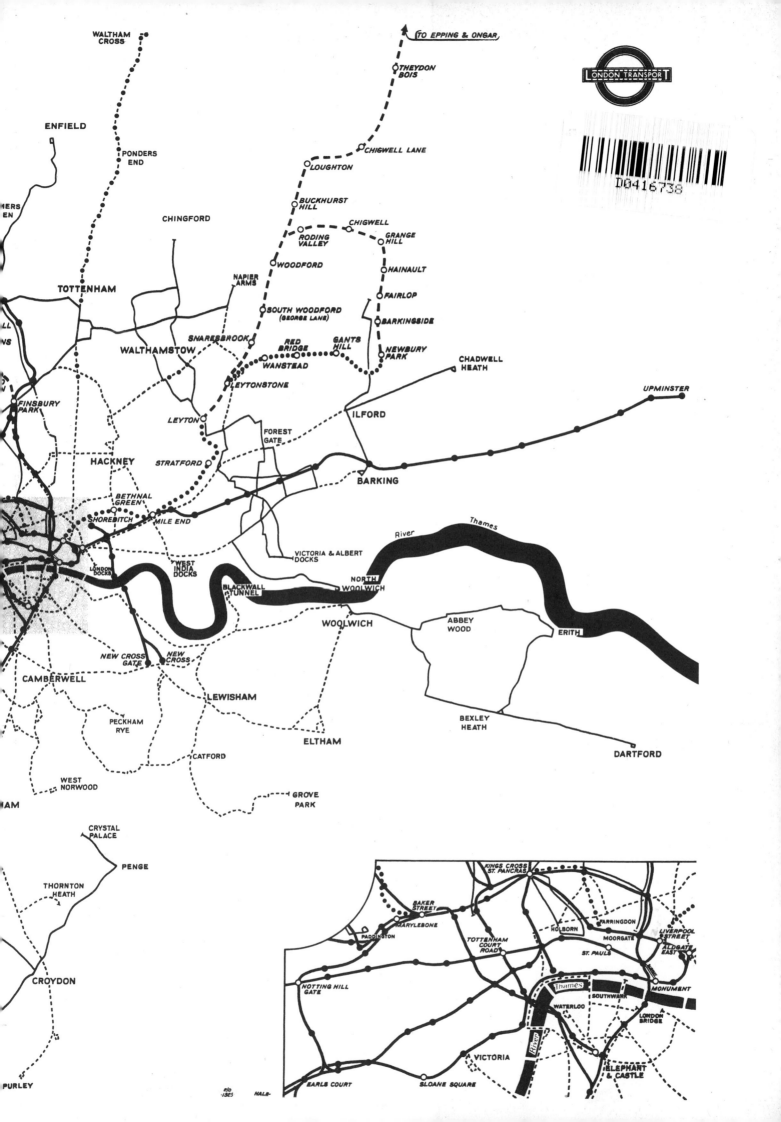

LONDON'S UNDERGROUND SUBURBS

· Dennis Edwards ·

· Ron Pigram ·

BLOOMSBURY BOOKS
LONDON

This book is dedicated to Ron Pigram who sadly died before seeing a finished copy. It is hoped it will be a fitting tribute to a man who loved his countryside and his means of transportation.

First published in 1986 by
BATON TRANSPORT
1 Russell Chambers
Covent Garden
London, WC2E 8AA

© Dennis Edwards and Ron Pigram 1986

This edition published 1988 by
Bloomsbury Books an imprint of
Godfrey Cave Associates Limited
42 Bloomsbury Street, London WC1B 3QJ
under license from Baton Transport/Cleveland Press

ISBN 1 870630 16 5

Printed in Yugoslavia

Other books by Dennis Edwards and Ron Pigram
The Metro-land trilogy:
Metro Memories
Romance of Metro-land
Golden Years of the Metropolitan Railway
The Final Link

Cover illustration
Golders Green. A railway poster of 1908, hinting at the ethereal domestic delights of rural Golders Green with the newly-opened Golders Green Underground station, complete with modern electric train, to be glimpsed in the background. The poster, by an unknown artist, bore a little rhyme which ended 'at a safe distance, where the dying sound falls a soft murmur upon the uninjured car'. Sound was quickly to increase as the district exploded in population with great speed.

Acknowledgements: The authors wish to thank the librarians and staff of museums in the London areas dealt with in this book, especially Hillingdon, Hounslow, Enfield, Ealing and the Chase Farm Museum, Hendon. We have also had unstinting assistance from Mr Hugh Davies (and his company staff) who was so involved in the developments in north London during the 1920s and 30s. To this we must add thanks to the Guildhall and Westminster Library, to the archive staff of London Regional Transport, the London Transport Museum, The Grange Museum, Neasden and Clive Smith of 'Memories', Hendon.

CONTENTS

INTRODUCTION

A multitude with spades and axes armed
To lay hills plain, fell woods, or valleys fill,
Or where plain raise hill, or over-lay
With bridge rivers proud . . .

Milton *Paradise Regained,* Book III

The expansion of London around the turn of the century was one of the most remarkable events of recent history. Heady with England's prosperity as the last golden flickers of sunlight fell upon that Victorian age of achievement, the great City continued to draw into itself more and more people. Slowly at first during Edwardian days, but then with increasing pressure, house building was undertaken in the immediate north and west London suburbs as this vast press of humanity struggled to live. Already south London had grown, but by the 1920s, as the men returned home from that terrible war in search of the land 'fit for heroes to live in', there emerged a growing awareness that their lives should alter in keeping with the new age. Everyone at least ought to have a roof over their head. And this undercurrent of social unease with the housing conditions of central London became so strong that the urge to have a home in the new suburbs became the major social event of that time. By a curious paradox, it all took place during times of great economic depression.

There were many forces at work. The strongest was the expansion of London's Underground railway system by men like Ashfield and Pick who were aggressively looking for more profitability for their public transport services. After the first World War the Tube lines were pushed out from London into open fields with complete assurance that the mass builder would buy up and develop every piece of nearby land for houses within months. Soon there was to be no stop to the housing momentum; there appeared to be endless green fields, and always the multitude of young couples who sought to move out of fly-infested London into the home of their dreams. Vast new housing estates strode out; newspaper advertising insistently offered houses for tiny deposits. However poor, it seemed as though almost everyone could afford to buy for the price of the rent they were paying each week. The media said that everything was suddenly possible; it was a brave new world populated with babies, mortgages and, of course, Mr Pick's smart new Underground trains.

Let us relax and take a look back over those days. First, we ask you to imagine the spirit and feel of those times – of fly-papers, meat safes, the heavy whirl of tram motors and grocers' shops where sugar and tea are weighed and popped into dark blue bags while you wait. A time of popping motor-cycles, but few cars, no television but one of wireless sets and wind-up gramophones. It is a world of music, so we'll pop on the latest Roy Fox record. On the new tiled Aztec fireplace, the dining-room clock is sounding the hours with its 'Westminster' chimes. Reach for the Abdulla cigarette and press the bronze statuette of the naked lady for a light.

Oh, and perhaps we have *just* time for a Green Goddess in one of these modern tall-stemmed cocktail glasses over there . . .

Ready? It is the moment to recall that Mr Chamberlain's 'piece of paper' will soon give us time to push Herr Hitler aside for a while and allow us to enjoy Noel Coward and his thoughts of

Cocktails and laughter,
But what comes after
Nobody knows!

7

GRASS ROUTES 1900-1914

In the autumn of 1900, two men drove in a hansom cab over the lofty heights of Hampstead Heath, high over London. From time to time the driver drew in his reins, allowing the men to leave and walk over the open spaces. Barely a rooftop could be seen. Later they took the cab down to see the level fields north of the hill. The only feature here was an isolated crossroads, fringed by a couple of old houses and some farm buildings. They had reached the rural hamlet of Golders Green, not far from Hendon.

The men were Charles Tyson Yerkes, and Harley Hugh Dalrymple Hay (who was later knighted). Yerkes (whose name was pronounced to rhyme with 'turkeys') was a financier from Chicago and had been described by the Press of the day as 'the Projector of the new Charing Cross, Euston and Hampstead Electric Underground'. His financial backing for the half-completed Tube railways of London, as well as his support of the District Railway, resulted in the formation of a parent company on 9 April 1902. It was the Underground Electric Railways Co Ltd, which became shortened later to the simple words 'Underground Group'.

Yerkes' little jaunt had a practical purpose, for he sought in that bleak land nothing less than space for a railway depot where, above ground, servicing and stabling for the Hampstead Tube could be built. Golders Green was just the place. But Dalrymple was not impressed. He saw only the lonely crossroads – who in their right mind would want to make the journey by train to visit such a spot?

Yerkes was built of stronger stuff. He had ambition. As early as 1896 he had met Dame Henrietta Barnett whilst on a voyage to Europe, and listened as she outlined her plans for a Garden Suburb near Hampstead. Gazing into her eyes, he confessed his own plans – to 'convey all London about in tunnels and this system of Underground travelling . . . would cause the erection of a station on the western edge of Hampstead Heath'. He rattled on

'A generation hence, London will be completely transformed, so that some people will think nothing of living 20 or more miles from Town owing to these electric railways.' Later, at an Enquiry on the Bill for the Golders Green extension, it was said that 'although Golders Green is but a short distance along the Finchley Road from the populous part of St John's Wood, . . . it is absolutely open country, for the simple reason that there is no means of getting to it'.

The extension was authorised under an Act of 18 November 1902, despite the protests of Hampstead people, who thought that the Tube tunnels under the Heath would act as a drain, so that all moisture would be led away and the trees and grass would die. The residents did win one big concession. There would be no station between Hampstead and Golders Green. As the Underground felt that this decision could eventually be over-ruled, work started on the platforms of an intermediate station at the 'Bull and Bush' – a public house that was immortalised in the music hall song by Florrie Forde. But the shafts from the surface were never sunk nor any buildings erected; the platforms remain unused to this day, although the space was used for wartime storage.

Work on the line began in September 1903 and was completed in December 1905, but much remained to be done before the trains could start running. Land was cleared at Golders Green for the Depot and the station. Yerkes never lived to see the public opening. He died at the Waldorf Astoria Hotel, New York, on 29 September 1905.

The Extension Line to Metro-land.
Of course, the Hampstead Tube was not the first London Underground railway to reach the countryside. The original underground line – the Metropolitan Railway – had extended out into the Middlesex countryside and on to the Chilterns in the 1880s as part of Sir Edward Watkin's grandiose scheme to

provide a route for his Great Central Railway Company (then the Manchester, Sheffield & Lincolnshire) to London and on to the south, the Channel Tunnel and Paris! (The story of the Metropolitan Railway and its Extension Line has been told in the authors' Metro-land Trilogy.)

The Extension Line sprang from the original single-tracked St John's Wood railway, which opened on 13 April 1868. The line was doubled in the 1870s and the first extension was by way of Finchley Road to West Hampstead. Originally, the St John's Wood promoters had high hopes of extending their line to Hampstead, but the railway was absorbed into the Metropolitan, and the route was to lead in another direction.

West Hampstead, in 1879, was still a semi-rural place. Indeed, so lonely and quiet was it that people were afraid to walk along West End Lane at night because of the dense hedges and overhanging trees. Yet within a few years the entire area was covered by rows of tall terraced houses and there was hardly an open space anywhere.

Kilburn had been known in the 18th century as Kilburn Wells, attracting the gentry and their ladies out from Georgian London. The Metropolitan Railway was extended beyond Kilburn to Harrow in 1880. An early railway guide book said that 'amongst the charms of Kilburn is its proximity to the countryside', a claim that even by 1890 would have been very hard to justify! Willesden Green was opened on 24 November 1879. 'Although at present there are so few houses in this locality, buildings are in course of formation and no doubt, considering the desirability of the site, and its easy communication with London, many more will follow, villas and houses to rent from £70 to £200pa,' the Guide Book predicted.

All the fields along the Edgware Road and south of the Metropolitan line quickly filled up with street after street of houses, the spread of houses eventually stretching as far north as Cricklewood. The Metropolitan Railway reached Harrow in 1880 and the land between the station, which is at the foot of the famous Hill, and the London & North Western line at Harrow and Wealdstone quickly filled up, absorbing the hamlet of Greenhill.

But it was at Northwood, a remote hamlet on the borders of Middlesex and Hertfordshire, that the first attempt was made on a new suburb. The station opened on 24 August 1887, but the new paint and its bright new gravel approaches attracted only a handful of travellers. So few passengers arrived in the early weeks that *The Times* reporter who braved the long journey from Baker Street said that the line was doomed to failure: 'People actually live in the neighbourhood and on Sunday last there were 250 on the train.'

Anticipating the possibilities that the new line might bring in house buyers, David Carnegie JP put his Eastbury Estate on the market on 25 March 1887. The estate was bought by Murray Maxwell Hallowell Carew, the son of an Admiral who had served as one of Nelson's captains. Carew offered building plots on 52 lots at his first sale. 'A rare opportunity for small capitalists and speculators to invest,' said the *Watford Observer*. Carew specified that the houses to be erected in Maxwell and Murray Roads should cost at least £750. At the other end of the social scale, he offered plots for the erection of cottages in High Street to cost not less than £120. A further ten land sales were held in the next few years and the roads were named after him and his family.

The Metropolitan Railway formed the Metropolitan Surplus Lands Committee on 30 June 1887. Unique amongst railways, the Met was able to grant legal powers to issue building licences and sell ground rents on its land. The Surplus Lands Committee promoted the first of the Metropolitan Railway estates at Cecil Park, Pinner, the first houses being built from 1900.

The Harrow & Uxbridge Railway. It was the opening of the Harrow and Uxbridge Railway in 1904 that was to be the stimulus to suburban

growth in the area which came to be called Metro-land. At the official opening lunch held in a vast marquee erected in the station yard at Uxbridge on 30 June, the Met's Chairman had predicted: 'Some of those persons here today will no doubt live to see the districts through which the new line passes, develop and furnish homes for London's ever-expanding population,' whilst the local press on that day described the village of Ruislip (when the only intermediate station on the line) as 'the sleepy hollow whose character will be gone; and the districts thus opened up will gradually take on the form of charming London suburbs'.

The first housing developments along this new railway, oddly enough, were at Ruislip! Under the Town and Country Planning Act of 1909, the Ruislip-Northwood Urban District Council held a competition for the planning of a garden city between Northwood and the area now known as South Ruislip. It called for an ambitious approach and the first prize was won by Westminster architects A & J Soutar. Their grand boulevard, landscaped Ruislip Reservoir and integrated groups of cottages, shops and villas, won great acclaim at an exhibition held in London.

'Ruislip-Northwood has placed the whole country under an obligation by being the first small authority to complete a town planning scheme,' said one newspaper. A company called Ruislip Manor Ltd was formed and its prospectus stated: 'Ruislip Manor Limited aims at introducing all classes into the community . . . but it is not intended to indiscriminately mix all classes and sizes of housing together, however.'

A few houses were completed before the first World War, but the original project was never revived, although the route of some of the principal roads was kept and the Ruislip Council maintained its high standards of planning control. The Ruislip that was eventually to emerge was a very different place to the dreams of 1904. The Council were greatly concerned with the

activities of a number of land developers who bought land near the Metropolitan Railway in the 1900s. The British Freehold Land Company sold plots for £3 down and 10s 0d (50p) per week. But buyers had to find their own builder and architect. So often they dispensed with the architect and designed their own homes, with disastrous results. It was a practice common in other areas, even after the war. The British Freehold Land Company tempted small investors: 'Try to own a suburban home; it will make you a better citizen and will help your family. The suburbs have fresh air, sunlight, roomy houses, green lawns and social advantages.'

Other local councils followed the Ruislip example and the Middlesex suburbs that were to grow a generation later were of brick houses with proper services and usually made-up roads. London's Underground suburbs were thus spared the shanty-town type sprawl that was to be a hallmark of many large cities in the United States.

In 1915 the Metropolitan Railway published the first of the famous series of *Metro-land* guides, (although it had published earlier railway guide books). In the very first issue, the Editor wrote: 'The strains which the London business or professional man has to endure amongst the turmoil and bustle of town can only be counter-balanced by the quiet restfulness and comfort of a residence in pure air and rural surroundings.'

Early developments west of Hammersmith. To the west of London, the Metropolitan District Railway (to give it its full title) had reached Hammersmith in 1874, thus competing with its old rival, the Metropolitan Railway, whose station lay just across the street. The District's publicity of the time claimed that its own station was 'superior in expedition and convenience to the Metropolitan Company's route from Moorgate Street'.

Further west, in just the same way that local business interests had taken the initiative in the Uxbridge area, Hounslow worthies in Victorian days had encouraged the idea of a rail service from their town into London. Nobody liked to be cut off in a small town. The first trains ran between Hounslow and a west London point known as Mill Hill Park (which became Acton Town from March 1910) as early as 1883. The District Railway, eyes cast firmly westwards, bought up this early railway, so giving some local pride in a permanent connection to Mansion House from the local terminus in Hounslow Town. However, in those days, with Ealing the top-class residential district (which had been served by the District since 1879), Hounslow was too far away from London to attract large-scale development by what we have come to call the 'commuter class.'

Hounslow's last period of importance dated from the days of the highwaymen and the coach links to Bath. Everything had gone a little to sleep since those times, although Hounslow Barracks, which had been built in 1793 for one cavalry regiment to give some protection against these robbers, gave continual demand for modern transport. When an infantry regiment was attached there, in 1875, a railway link had to be only years away.

A new station, called reasonably enough, Hounslow Barracks, appeared on the Bath Road in July 1884, leaving the original terminus station out, literally, 'on a limb'. There had to be a complicated shunting operation to serve both places, and it was no surprise when less than two years later, the Hounslow Town station was abandoned for another new station on the Barracks line. This new structure was called Heston-Hounslow, in a cunning attempt to attract custom from the small village of Heston which then lay, hidden by trees, about half-an-hour's walk away to the north.

Hounslow Town, after its closure in March 1886, remained so until 1903. It reopened for six years, but finally closed in 1909, the site becoming part of the land attaching to Hounslow bus garage.

The District Railway had also a short spur line which ran from Earl's Court to West Brompton. Railway expansion was the order of the day, and in March 1880 the lines were pushed beyond West Brompton to Putney Bridge. An agreement was reached with the London & South Western Railway for a further extension to Surbiton, and the main-line company spanned the Thames with a massive bridge and carried District trains to Wimbledon which had its first District Railway service from June 1889. There was also an agreement with the main-line railway to use the LSWR lines from Ravenscourt Park to Richmond. A short connecting spur was all that was needed from Hammersmith, allowing yet another town, Richmond, to be 'plugged in' to the District in June 1877.

In 1877, too, came London's first true Garden Suburb – Bedford Park. It was built beside Turnham Green station and was designed by Jonathan Carr. The best architects of the day were employed there – Norman Shaw, who had created New Scotland Yard; Charles F. A. Voysey, a little man of genius who was to create a very individual style of homes in the Misbourne valley; and others of almost equal merit. They fashioned the houses which had to be 'in the right place for the people of the right type' in a Queen Anne style. It was very much a creation for the rich and upper middle class, with rents *from* £40 a year. Here, in Bedford Park, was a church and an inn – the 'Tabard' – so that the residents should want for little other mortal comfort; as well as 'institutes for social life' as the estate was, at that time, thought to be rather remote from the hurly-burly of fashionable London life.

Bedford Park was very advanced for its day, and was well criticised, it being alleged that 'it is the suburb for the artistic bourgeoisie', a view that we may, with the advantage of another age, tend to agree with. There was even a poem about the estate, in the style of Chaucer:

Thus was a village builded
For all who are aesthete

Whose precious souls it fill did
With other joys complete.
(*Ballad of Bedford Park,* 1881)

A resident told one of the weekly magazine reporters of the time that he felt he was living in some water colour painting of the rural romantic school!

Everybody had a garden and for a time the estate produced its own newspaper. Houses quickly filled the flat fields between Kew Gardens and near the railway towards Richmond, also the market gardens at Gunnersbury.

Along the Wimbledon Line things were happening fast. By 1895 H. S. Vaughan in *The Way About Middlesex* wrote: 'Twenty years ago there was a pleasant country road from Walham Green, bordered by fields, market gardens and nurseries, and grounds with many fruit trees.' He was writing amid a sea of new houses. The success of the District's extensions into south-west London were said to have brought 'health and betterment to the inhabitants of London'.

Houses 'like several battalions of a gigantic army, marching and counter marching' were spreading over the south Middlesex fields. By the end of the 19th century most of the land between West Brompton, Hammersmith and Chiswick was developed and Ealing was already earning its title as 'The Queen of Suburbs'. The steam trains and their uncomfortable carriages were becoming an embarrassment to the District Railway and were soon to be discarded.

The District Railway became part of the 'Underground Group' in 1901 but before that the Ealing & South Harrow Railway had been incorporated in 1894 as part of the District's ambitions to reach Uxbridge. The line was constructed in 1899, but no trains ran on this extension until the pioneer electrification of 1903. The very first section of the District's 'surface' Underground to be electrically worked opened on 23 June 1903 between Mill Hill Park (Acton Town) and Park Royal for the Royal Agricultural Society's show. Heavy rains had caused some earth slip further north and it was not until 28 June that trains could work to South Harrow. Sidings were laid down for the new electric trains, which looked very American in design.

The Met's Harrow & Uxbridge Railway had built a viaduct to South Harrow from Rayners Lane, but there were no passenger trains to connect the two lines until the District began its service to Uxbridge in 1910. It was this rather quiet branch line, through Sudbury and Alperton to South Harrow and rural Rayners Lane, that was to become the route of the Piccadilly Line's westward extension in 1933.

The Hampstead Tube arrives. We began our story with some early facts about Golders Green and how the hamlet became the first Tube railway suburb.

Trains began on Saturday 22 June 1907, the service being officially opened by the President of the Board of Trade, Lloyd George. The services ran from Charing Cross to either Golders Green or Highgate (the junction for the two northern branches being at Camden Town). Travel on that first day was free and advertisements all over London announced: 'The Last Link . . . in the chain of communication . . . of a complete system of underground railway transit which it is believed will not only help to solve the pressing problem of street congestion, but will introduce wide reaching changes in the distribution of population, the location of shopping centres and the travel habits of the people.'

In the next few years great changes *were* to come about at the hamlet of Golders Green! Even in the years shortly before the building of the line, the local authority, Hendon Council, had opened a new Town Hall in the centre of old Hendon village; the famous Golders Green Crematorium (then an extremely novel idea for disposing of the dead) was opened in 1905. Street lamps appeared along the Finchley Road about this time and two estate agents set up their huts in a field near the proposed terminus in October 1905.

The passing of the Edgware &

Hampstead Railway Act of 18 November 1902 and the Watford & Edgware Railway Act of the same year stimulated speculation that housing development would soon take place. There was an immediate improvement in communications to distant Edgware with the Metropolitan Electric Tramway Company's electric trams' arrival in 1906. A further extension of the tramway took place to Canons Park, further north along the Edgware Road, in October 1907.

By October 1905, the first house stood completed at the corner of Finchley Road and Hoop Lane, Golders Green. In the following year a visitor to the area commented: 'Within sight of the Golders Green terminus of the Hampstead Tube, half-a-dozen estate agents' pavilions may be counted dotted about the fields.'

After the line opened, the growth of Golders Green was rapid. By the end of 1907 there were 73 houses. In 1914 there were 471. New roads such as The Grove, The Drive, Templar's Avenue and Wentworth Road, were built and all day long there was a continuous hammering like the sound of distant thunder as the armies of carpenters got to work.

Not far from Golders Green, Hampstead Garden Suburb was being built under the Hampstead Garden Suburb Act of 1906. The village was the idea, as we have seen, of Dame Henrietta Barnett, being 'a place where poor shall teach the rich and where the rich, let us hope, shall help the poor to help themselves'. A set of rules or objectives were drawn up in the prospectus for the estate; and among them were:
(a) That persons of all classes of society and standards of income shall be accommo-dated and that the handi-capped be welcomed.
(b) That the cottages and houses should be limited to an average of eight to an acre.
(c) Roads are to be 40ft wide and lined with trees.
Noise was to be avoided even to the prohibiting of Church, Chapel or Institute bells.

Lower ground rents were to be

charged in certain areas 'to enable weekly wage earners to live on the estate'.

The houses were to be so planned 'that none shall spoil each other's outlook or rob its neighbour of beauty'.

The architects of the buildings included Edward Lutyens, C. Cowles, C. A. Voysey, Geoffrey Lucas and W. Curtis-Green. There were churches and a library. But the roads were too narrow for public transport and the suburb's carefully planned atmosphere of 'safety and enclosure' proved too much for the working-class residents, who soon abandoned their homes to the middle classes and moved back to the relative chuminess of the inner suburbs. Later the peace of the area was to be broken by the construction, across the southern edge, of the Hendon by-pass.

Off to Watford by Bakerloo. The London & North Western Railway had for years neglected the potential of suburban traffic along its main line out of Euston, and for a long while the station at Willesden Junction, where the North London Railway crossed over the main line, was called 'The Wilderness'. But London expanded through Kilburn and Queen's Park towards Willesden. The arrival of the Metropolitan Railway to the north of this area also stimulated housing. Queen's Park was laid out as a model of working-class housing and the actual public park itself was opened on 5 May 1887 by Sir Reginald Hanson. Beyond Willesden Junction there were scruffy fields, and the once-rural surroundings that had been painted earlier in that century by the artist Morland were further spoiled by the building of the LNWR's vast sidings at Stonebridge Park. Yet, in 1875, a development here of sixty or so new villas had been described as ideal homes for City men!

It was the arrival of the Bakerloo Line that was to open up this part of London for development. The original Baker Street & Waterloo Railway (the name Bakerloo was coined by the

Evening News writer 'Quex') opened on Saturday 10 March 1906. A short extension opened from Baker Street to Marylebone on 27 March 1907 to link with the newly built Great Central. Sir Sam Fay of the Great Central wanted the Tube station simply called 'Great Central'. The line was pushed on to Edgware Road on 15 June 1907 and to Paddington on 1 December 1908. Powers were obtained in 1911–12 for an extension from here to the surface and alongside the LNWR lines to Queen's Park and beyond. Labour troubles caused by the first World War delayed the completion and the new line did not open until 11 February 1915. In May of that year some trial trips were made along the electrified tracks as far as Willesden Junction, and to Kensal Green on October 1916. The LNWR had already laid a pair of additional tracks out as far as Watford Junction, with a loop line round Watford via Bushey and High Street, worked by a steam service from 1915.

It was planned that LNWR electric trains would eventually use the tracks, with an underground terminus beneath the main line station at Euston. It was intended to start the joint electric service with the Bakerloo northwards from Queen's Park but, because of the war, the LNWR electric trains were not ready.

The Bakerloo Railway was equipped with additional rolling stock which was specially built for the long run into the countryside – luggage racks and comfortable seats. The external livery was in the LNWR colours instead of traditional Underground red and cream. The trains finally began running to Watford Junction from Elephant & Castle on 16 April 1917. The journey was then the longest on the Tube lines – 21 miles.

Some housing developments took place at Wembley, Harrow & Wealdstone, and Hatch End before 1914. The Avenue and Roslyn Park areas of Hatch End were popular with City men. Some of the stations were rebuilt, with booking halls designed by C. Horsley.

The Ealing & Shepherd's Bush Railway. On 14 May 1908 the Central London Railway, (the original 'tuppenny Tube') was extended from Shepherd's Bush to Wood Lane to serve the Franco-British Exhibition which opened that year at White City. Over the next few years the line carried vast crowds to the series of international exhibitions held at White City. There were plans to extend the railway to Richmond (powers were actually obtained under an Act of 15 April 1913). But it was in conjunction with the Great Western Railway's Ealing and Shepherd's Bush Railway Act of 10 April 1917 that the Tube line was eventually to reach Ealing Broadway and rival the District for the upper middle-class passengers from that 'Queen of suburbs'. The first World War prevented progress with the project.

Life in the Edwardian city. Apart from the rather grand pioneer developments along the route of the Metropolitan Railway, most middle and lower middle-class Londoners in the Edwardian Age lived in places on the fringe of the central area – places such as Wood Green, Kilburn, Willesden, Ealing, Finsbury Park and Dalston.

The average family rented a house; most rented *part* of one, or often just a room or two. Few owned property, and the mortgage fashion was a long way off. Borrowing required regular income.

Most of the Edwardian suburbs consisted of long streets of terraced red or yellow London-bricked houses, with projecting bay windows, mullioned in stone, that overlooked small handkerchief-sized front gardens. The rear of some of the larger houses had a slate-roofed extension covering the kitchen and sometimes a lavatory. Bathrooms started to appear after 1890. A straggle of privet separated the occupants of the house from the noise and dirt of the street, and afforded a little sparse privacy in densely-packed surroundings. At the rear of these inner London houses was a small yard, perhaps even a tiny garden.

Very often, from a convenient large nail driven into the wooden fence, a long zinc bath hung in view, ready for use on washday, and for the very occasional hot bath which was taken, in those houses without bathrooms, in front of a large fire after the bath had been filled with water heated in kettles.

The outside of most houses presented a universally dismal view, for brown paint was the order of the day. It was tidy, did not 'shout', and did not show the dirt so much as any other shade. The London fogs ate deeply into the lead composition of the material covering the wooden sills. A few brave hearts, who wanted to be 'different', painted their houses black and white, or black and cream. It was regarded by the neighbours as very advanced, and 'something to do with the Dutch'.

The Victorians, with their instinct for concealment, preferred blinds at the front windows, and lace curtains, too. The parlour or 'front room' was kept for visitors, or for Christmas celebrations. Most people had a granny or granddad living with them (because of the fear of the 'workhouse'), and there were many (including animals) crammed into a very small area. Walls were dark and varnished, especially on the staircases where it was 'difficult to do'. Wallpapers were heavily patterned in large floral designs. Flypapers hung in the kitchens.

Yet, despite common belief that things were not much different from the Victorian times, the Edwardian home had progressed, with carpets (where possible), and coloured lino.

Not everybody, by any means, actually *had* a kitchen (some made do with a gas ring on the half-landing) but there were no machines to help speed the grind of the day other than an occasional clothes drier which was fixed to the ceiling and could be lowered to dry clothes in the fug of the room.

With the first 'cat's-whisker' wireless set appearing only in the early Twenties, entertainment before that time was very much up to the individual. Most people played an instrument and usually enough money could be scraped together to buy a small gramophone – that amazing new marvel!

And during these early years in the Underground suburbs (reached by bus or tram if they were any distance from the centre of London), there was always the *local* music hall. It was, after all, a *part* of London, with rich luxuriously decorated interiors – a riot of gold and crimson. Fred Matcham, who also decorated the early cinemas, was a leading music-hall designer of the time.

But these tended to be winter pastimes – on summer days the call of 'Appy 'Ampstead delighted the kids and it was only a short Tube or bus ride away for most people. The newly electrified Metropolitan and District Railways encouraged the desire to spend the day further afield – to Richmond perhaps, by the river. Or a walk to see the windmill on Wimbledon Common. For middle-class children, it was no longer satisfying to have

A tuppeny ride on a tramcar
   Down to Victoria Park,
A tuppeny ride on a donkey
   To show I was having a lark.

The call of the open air. The days of the great School Treat were still with us in the 1900s – a Victorian children's outing for a year of good attendance at Sunday School or day school – and went on well into the Thirties.

In west London children were taken on highly organised outings (some financed by local traders) to the countryside at Ruislip or Eastcote. The Pavilion Gardens specially catered for such parties in the Twenties – there was a large area at Field End Road, Eastcote, set aside for picnics, rounders, donkey rides and roundabouts (and there was cover for over 4,000 people if it started to rain). The Ruislip tea gardens of The Poplars was a favourite, while other school parties got as far as High Wycombe, Oxshott Woods in south London and, of course, that great wooded area for East Londoners – Epping Forest.

The open-air life blossomed for adults too, but this was mostly confined to their only 'spare' day – Sunday. The Golders Green fields were popular in early days, whilst anglers travelled into Middlesex to streams around Uxbridge, or out to fish the Kingsbury reservoir, making for the famous old pub, the 'Welsh Harp', on the Edgware Road, to swap fishing stories. The reservoir itself became known as the 'Welsh Harp'.

Trams were packed with family groups as they trundled out along the Metropolitan electric track from Cricklewood and Willesden to Edgware and Canons Park. The new Hampstead Tube had to lengthen the Sunday trains on its route from four to six cars in the summer. This, in turn, brought out a new rash of posters – most of them very attractive and carrying the legend 'Book to Hampstead or Golders Green'. The District Railway, which from 1 June 1910 had started running 'through' trains daily from Ealing to Southend-on-Sea, was not to be outdone, and some attractive seaside scenes appeared on its posters. Trains consisted of special sets of London Tilbury & Southend Railway carriages, which were hauled by electric locomotives as far east as Barking.

There was even a tame local band which played in the forecourt of Golders Green Station as the crowds queued for buses to take them home to London! Some who waited had walked over the fields from Hendon, following a leaflet issued by the 'General' Bus company, which started 'from the swing gate at the meadows beside Hendon church . . .'

All these changes in social behaviour for Londoners were taking place slowly over the years. There was not too much spare money around for bus and train rides, but there was a general feeling that it was healthy to get out into the open air when possible. A number of activists were urging concern about the public living standards. The Boer War had found recruits to have a very low physical standard, pointing to widespread lack of proper food and living conditions.

Ebenezer Howard, with his Golden City dream at Letchworth and his book *Garden Cities of Tomorrow*, had also given a bold lead in the direction that, ideally, Londoners should be heading.

With the constant child loss through diphtheria and scarlet fever – major killer diseases in the early 1900s until the second World War – there was an unconscious unrest about the way that most Londoners were forced to live. Everyone wanted clean country air for their children, clean country air. 'Overcrowding is dangerous – the air in densely crowded areas becomes germ-laden,' Government reports conceded. Just before the first World War the national newspapers were urging better housing, and a world where 'the fresh air of the country districts will be available to all . . . where the slums are gone and where modern sanitation excels'.

The new network of Underground railways after the war was to provide some of the answers, and bring a new way of life for millions who could use them to separate their work in London from their homes. The railways were to break down much of the class reserves, although 'First Class' was to persist on the surface lines until after all the dreams of new housing were starting to fade with the threat of another war.

In the rough jostle of rush hours on the Tube lines, and the push to get a seat home on a tram or bus for the rest of the journey, everyone took their own chance. It was still polite to offer a lady a seat on the Tube, but there were very few women travelling compared to the thousands of men, and there were nasty scenes at many of the tube/bus/tram interchanges almost daily.

With the outbreak of the second World War, the urge for new homes came to a stop. 'The bomber will always get through,' it was said, and everything could be lost in a flash. It had been much the same at the outbreak of the first World War, though without real air threat. Between those two terrible world events, London's green countryside changed almost overnight into a vast area of houses in all directions.

Homes for heroes. After the first World War the slogan 'a land fit for heroes' was on every politician's lips. Men were just not prepared to go back to a life of despair – to own their own home was the dream of most ex-servicemen – not just the middle classes but the working-class men as well.

The Metropolitan Railway seemed to be always ready; the General Manager, Selbie, wrote in 1918· 'In view of the large demand there will be for houses as soon as Peace is declared, and the forces are demobilised . . . I am of the opinion that the scheme of forming an Estates Company (to develop the spare land beside the railway tracks for housing) should be taken in hand forthwith.'

For north-west London, the result was the Metropolitan Railway Estates Company, formed in 1919. It had originated 'not merely to provide superior houses in the rural countryside near London, but also to create new passenger traffic'. Here was the early clue to the railway companies' extreme interest in home development. Very few houses, however, were built in the early Twenties due to the aftermath of the war, shortages of skilled materials and labour, as well as national exhaustion. Everywhere they were erecting the memorial crosses for the dead.

But in a few years things started to move with the resumption by the Government in 1923 of private subsidies, so that developers could raise the capital to purchase land. The *Architectural Journal* of this time found that 'thanks to private enterprise . . . estates are springing up on the outskirts of London which promise to meet an urgent need'.

Middlesex, flat and sparsely populated, attracted many builders. There were exceptional public transport facilities to Uxbridge, Hounslow and the Thames-side at Twickenham by District, Metropolitan and Southern Railway trains. It was here, according to the *Evening News* in 1933, that there was 'a solution for the desire of people to

live in more rural surroundings and away from the noise of London traffic'. And in the same year, the Middlesex County Officer for Health commented on the influence that the Underground railway was having on the county, enhancing its growth, and bringing inaccessible parts within easy reach of London: 'The builder has followed hard upon the improvement in transport and is rapidly transforming the remaining rural parts of Middlesex into urban communities.'

Thoroughly modern. During the Thirties builders offered all kinds of inducements to buy. It was bewildering and very exciting. There were free tickets to visit the new estates by Underground, and most house builders offered interior decoration to choice. Some of the more expensive houses had 'fitted kitchens'. Black-and-white dado tiles broke up the sanitary white of the new bathrooms. The great London stores offered a wide array of furniture. The range of house designs was wide, and within the financial reach of most young marrieds struggling to keep their heads above water during the depressions of the early Thirties. Osbert Lancaster lampooned the London suburbs of the day with a series of cartoons depicting styles such as 'Modernisk', 'By-Pass Variegated' and 'Wimbledon Transitional'. It was the age of *Art Deco* – in these homes 'radios lurked in tea caddies and bronze nudes burst asunder at the waistline to reveal cigarette lighters. Nothing is what it seems'. J. B. Priestley saw how people went to look over 'these new houses, seeing them as a kind of signpost pointing to a sunlit main road of life'.

Although the economic depression had hit London hard, things improved quicker in London and south-eastern England than elsewhere. By 1936 unemployment in Middlesex, with its new factories along the Great West Road, was down to 4.5%, a figure to be compared to Glamorgan with 33.4%. The new factories brought more people who, once they had a regular job, could start to look

around for a house with only £25 in their pockets.

Inside the new home, London furnishers had immediate solutions: Waring & Gillow bedroom suites for £10 10s (£10.50p) complete with triple-glassed dressing table for the bay window. For the kitchen, Catesby of London offered a kitchen cabinet with glass doors for under £5; the cabinet being filled with free packets of Hudson's Soap Powder, Lux Flakes, and the new Oxydol. There was also a packet of Cadbury's Drinking Chocolate for a night-cap.

Kitchens were equally important as the centre of the weekly wash. Most builders offered free boilers. Refrigerators were so rare that anyone claiming to have one would be besieged by neighbours seeking to keep some perishable luxury in such safety!

The 1930s were years of innovation and rapid change. Fashion designs were fluid; it was the age of car dicky-seats, sun motifs, and streaming hair on everything – including stained glass and cigarette packets as well as soap packets. Some have tried to equate the rising sun and the youthful figures of *Art Deco* design with the spirit of *Jugendherben*, particularly after 1933 with the rise of the Nazi party in Germany. It was an age when it was good to be young; not to look forward to the future, even though things appeared better than just after 1918. It was a time to try to enjoy oneself.

Temples of escapism. The cinema, with the advent of the talkie age, became the most important building in London's suburbs. 'The cinema fills a need in our lives which no preceding age has ever felt,' confided F. Morton Shand in 1930, before the real explosion of the cinema took place. C. Day Lewis' remark about 'cinemas before churches' reflected the feeling – simple wooden huts often served as new parish churches for the growing estates around London.

Cinemas, in fact, became the social centres of the times. With seats for matinees as low as 4d (1½p) if you queued early, everyone could afford escapism in those days without television. Housewives, most of whom were without jobs apart from looking after their children, slipped away for a quiet cry at Hollywood love dramas in the darkness of the cinema; on Saturdays, with the children, there was the delight of the mighty Würlitzer organ resurrecting itself out of the cinema pit during the interval when Eldorado ice-cream was on sale. There was also live entertainment on the cinema stage on occasions. And, when it was all over, there were the cheerful red Underground trains to whisk the family back home.

Soon every London suburb, however new, had its Granada, Rex or Odeon. The name 'Odeon' has no classical association – it stood simply for Oscar Deutsch Entertains Our Nation. Thirty-four new places opened in 1936 alone. Deutsch, the company Head, kept Harry Weedon, his leading architect, busy designing medium-sized buildings which dwarfed the places around them. They were beacons of the new bright age, leaving thoughts of suburban days in muddy, foggy streets far behind for ever.

> Enter the dream house, brothers
>   and sisters,
> Leaving
> Your debts asleep, your history at
>   the door,
> This is the house for heroes, and
>   this loving
> Darkness a fur you can afford . . .
>
> . . . Sleep walking on that silver
>   wall, the furious
> Sick shapes and pregnant fancies
>   of your world.
>   (C. Day Lewis: *Newsreel*, 1938)

Inviting doorways. But if the cinemas were temples of entertainment, the Underground stations were the temples of travel. Frank Pick, Vice-Chairman of the Underground Group, had called his stations 'inviting doorways in an architectural setting that cannot be missed by the casual passer-by'.

To live near an Underground station was considered by many people to be 'the acme of convenience'. The newer station buildings were designed to be wide and welcoming; the trains so frequent that you didn't need a timetable; and the fares cheap enough for all. There were the well-lit, colourful Underground trains and the platforms with their artistic posters that provided a never-ending source of delight as they poured out from 55 Broadway year after year. No wonder people would walk miles to reach the Underground. Frank Pick and Charles Holden, his Architect, had taken a trip round Northern Europe in the 1920s, and in consequence the use of concrete, bronze and large windows became features of the Underground architecture.

Pick commissioned Edward Johnson to design a special type-face in 1916, to be used on Underground signs and publicity, and his attention to every detail of design and function became legendary.

The Underground was seen as the safe, swift way around London during the Thirties. It was the gateway to the pleasures of the West End. 'To Town Tonight' was a publicity theme of Underground advertising for many years. London's hundreds of cinemas, theatres, concert halls, sports events, to say nothing of the cafes, restaurants and great stores, the exhibitions, circuses and pageantry, offered a seemingly endless variety of entertainments.

The department stores had their origins in the late 19th century. It was not until the period just before 1914 that they became places where ladies could spend a day safely and unchaperoned. Stores opened restaurants and cafes where ladies, mothers and children from the new suburbs could feel safe from whatever horrors Edwardian patresfamilias imagined awaited their unaccompanied womenfolk in the West End streets. The new stores were among the first public places to provide ladies' rooms – something that previously had been provided only at hotels.

But after about 1937 there appears to have been a slackening off in evening travel to London. Homes were becoming more comfortable. The suburbs were beginning to mature and offer social clubs, churches and cinemas. The demands of children and gardens kept people more at home on Saturdays. The wireless set became universal and the younger families could now listen to commercial stations such as Radio Luxembourg (1934) and Radio Normandy.

The perpetual expansion of London – from Bedford to Brighton and Southend to Reading – was slowing down at last.

The Green Belt. As early as 1932, the Middlesex County Council had paid £226,000 towards the cost of buying a portion of countryside near Hendon for Green Belt. Sir Montague Barlow's Royal Commission on the growth of London (1938) laid the foundations of the Green Belt ideal. Despite the LPTB's New Works Programmes 1935–6 with their grandiose schemes for Northern Line expansions to Elstree, and Central Line west to Denham, and Ongar in the east, the days were coming to an end for endless suburbs.

It was after the second World War that the Green Belt Plan became fact. Based on the Abercrombie Greater London Development Plan, the final curb on expansion into the countryside came with the Town and Country Planning Act 1947.

But there were other curbs on the development of Underground suburbs by 1938. Builders were indeed anticipating the arrival of the Central Line to Ruislip and Denham and some building was taking place at Northolt, Greenford and south Ruislip. The first parades of shops went up at Denham near the film studios, but there was a reluctance to start really large estates. The very last estates advertising feature in the *Evening News* of 26 August 1939 announced 'the pick of the safety zones' for new houses outside the central and southern areas of London.

Many of the empty houses and flats were quickly filled in 1940 by people who were 'bombed out'. The unexpected sirens of Sunday 3 September 1939 sounded the end of the Underground suburbs.

Dollis Hill Lane. A scene early this century, when there was still countryside at the edge of the built-up area around Willesden Green and Dollis Hill.

South Harrow. Fun and teas at The Paddocks gardens about 1912. Right up until the late 1920s, Mr A. B. Champniss had 30 acres of grounds around his villa in Northolt Road near Northolt Park station laid out with amusements, plus donkey rides and sports, for 3,000 visitors. Children and adults marched down the road from South Harrow station to spend a memorable day here beneath the oaks and elms. Gradually the suburbs caught up with South Harrow and the lands were sold for development. Fortunately, some of the land was incorporated in Alexandra Park in 1936.

In the City. Every suburban breadwinner was 'Something in the City' and here are some of them waiting for the trains home at Aldersgate & Barbican before 1914. An Inner Circle train is arriving, whilst the steam train is on the Midland Railway, running on the Metropolitan's Widened Lines.

High Road, Willesden Green.

Willesden Green. It was from crowded streets, like this view of High Road, near the Metropolitan station that people went out to live in the more attractive green suburbs along the extensions of the Underground. This scene dates from about 1910.

Pleasure traffic.
This early poster was one of a series drawn for the Underground Group by Mabel Lucy Attwell.

Horse-bus depot. A London horse-bus depot of the 1890s, with cars ready to ply to Islington and the slowly developing districts of Hampstead. Headgear is *de rigueur*, and used informally to convey status from the bowler-hatted Foremen to the cloth caps of the ancilliary shift workers.

Highbury & Islington. The station, seen four months or so after the formation of the London Passenger Transport Board in 1933. Although the Met had managed to get the station name carried on the periphery brickwork, there is still a 'hang-dog' appearance that was common to so many other Tube stations at the time, and which made the drastic architectural experiments of the extension stations so much more exciting. Here was London in the days of heat, grinding tram wheels, and flies.

12   CLAPHAM. — High Street. — LL.

Clapham. A busy day in Clapham High Street in Edwardian Days! Everything was here for the average Londoner – Oxford University was playing at The Oval – only a couple of stations away by the electric Tube on the City & South London Railway, which had opened just more than a decade earlier, and was now competing with the fast electric trams.

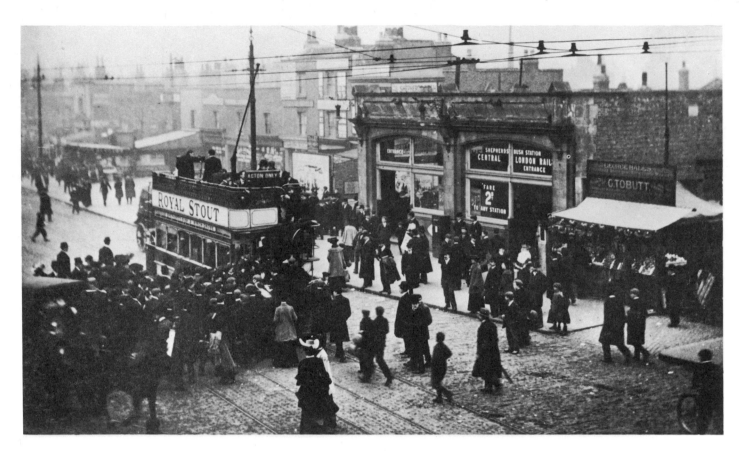

Shepherd's Bush. Start of the evening rush hour? This is, in fact, an early afternoon photograph (2.55pm) taken on 21 March 1905 at Shepherd's Bush, as the crowd surge into the centre of the main road to board the Acton tram. Fortunately, there is little traffic, although a horse-and-cart, concealed by the vehicle, presents a danger which is ignored. Trams did, in fact, present constant hazards because of their inability to draw up beside the curb.

Perhaps a train has just arrived at the station, whose buildings forming the station front appear to be almost any ordinary shop, except for the painted advertisements upon glass. This was the original 'tuppenny' Tube, as the fare tariff shows.

Shepherd's Bush (Central London Railway). Another view, taken a little earlier, of this early major west London train-tram interchange.

Shepherd's Bush. Rare early view of the Central London platforms when they were the terminus of the 'tuppenny' Tube (the flat fare all the way from the Bank). The wooden platforms and the newspaper stand (just visible in the background) are lit by flash powder thrown by the photographer's assistant.

Ealing. Every large Edwardian suburb had its music hall. The 'reputable family' entertainment at the Ealing Hippodrome ensured that the suburban family of respectability did not risk their morals by hearing Marie Lloyd! The Hippodrome replaced the old Lyric Hall in 1899. Later the theatre became the Palladium Cinema and lasted until the late 1950s. W. H. Smith's store on the site incorporates the old under-stage scenery dock in its basement!

Ealing Broadway. By the time the District Railway was electrified to Ealing Broadway, the area had become an important suburban shopping centre. Crowds are waiting for one of the LUT's trams approaching on the route to Shepherd's Bush. Over Fosters, the outfitters (the firm was here until the beginning of the 1980s), is an American dentist, but no doubt the cries of his patients were drowned by the grinding trams, and the rattle of the horse-drawn traffic. The turret in the middle distance is that of the Hippodrome Theatre.

Ealing. Highview Road about 1902, with a steam traction 'road train' of supplies for building new houses.

Kilburn. Metropolitan Extension Line train shortly before electrification of the line. Great Central tracks are to the right. The Beyer Peacock locomotive is No. 34, which was sold to Bradford Corporation in 1905, and then in 1914 to the Welsh Granite Company. The houses under construction were available at rents from £70 per year. 'The houses now being constructed are of singular convenience and as to style, expertly tailored . . .' said the builder's prospectus.

Hendon. Looking down Greyhound Hill, with a pioneer flying machine about to make a landing at Hendon Aerodrome, then called 'The London Aerodrome'. The old signpost points the way to rural Page Street and Mill Hill.

Earl's Court Wheel. The series of exhibitions held at Earl's Court on land owned by the District Railway ran from 9 May 1887 until 1913. The big wheel was a landmark from 1895 until 1906.

Acton Town. The original station was opened on 1 July 1879 as Mill Hill Park. This view dates from the end of the 19th century. The growth of traffic eventually led to rebuilding with extra tracks and the station was named Acton Town from 1910. The station was rebuilt in 1932, ready for the Piccadilly Line western extensions.

Merton Road and Theatre, Wimbledon.

Wimbledon. A street scene of the mid-Twenties with little vehicular activity, other than the electric tram in the background. There are local cyclists, who were well advised to keep clear of the dangers from the tram tracks and stone road sets which could give rise to bad accidents.

Special treat. A London kiddies outing – a popular local event usually organised by charities, in this case the local busmen. The time is August 1926. Most of the local population has turned out early in the morning to see off the busloads of excited schoolchildren in the 'B' open-top buses. The open charabanc in the foreground usually ran on the coach excursions of the London General Omnibus Company to the surrounding countryside. The local bus garage was Dalston.

Hampstead. The Tube station shortly after it opened in 1907. The platforms are 192ft below the surface – the deepest on the Underground system.

Golders Green. The Depot for the Hampstead Tube lines, in the late 1920s, with 'Standard' stock trains.

Golders Green. The station, when first opened in 1907. 'Tube now Open' proclaims the banner, but no passengers are around, and only a couple of horse-drawn carriages await the arrival of their owners on the London train.

Golders Green. All clean and new at the terminus. The horse-bus is probably one of those running up to The Bell at Hendon (until 8.36pm weekdays and 9.12pm on Sundays). The tree on the left has been preserved by building the bus shelter roof around it!

Golders Green. No other Underground suburb had as good a Tube train service as Golders Green. From 1909 a businessmen's non-stop train was run to Euston, passing Belsize Park and some other stations. It was so successful that non-stop trains were then run at certain off-peak times as well. There were also theatre non-stop trains from October 1910, leaving Golders Green at 7.16pm, arriving at Leicester Square in 14 minutes. The return train left the West End at 11.15pm. The train in this picture was photographed on 13 November 1911.

Golders Green. Work on the Woodstock Estate, Golders Green, near the turn of the century. This scene, showing concrete sewer construction, was taken in 1908. The man in the boater is Howard Farrow, co-founder of the firm of Howard Farrow Construction Ltd.

Near Barnet. A 'General' open-top 'B' bus at Barnet crossroads on its way to St Albans about the time of the first World War. Route 84 was, for many years after the removal of the London Transport Country Bus department in 1970, unique in its continuous 'red bus' link to St Albans Country Bus Garage.

Golders Green. The open country at Golders Green soon after the Hampstead Tube line had reached the district. This shows most graphically the rural scene at that time, repeated throughout the environs of London. No one (other than a ghostly policeman beyond the hedgeline) is to be seen on this dreary, rain-sodden road. But the lane on the left leads to the new station booking office, and the estate developers (Raymond & Crump), vie with Ernest Owers, another estate agent who has taken over the only building that can be seen.

Northwood. Pioneer Metro-land suburb of the 1880s: this old postcard shows the new shops in Maxwell Road about 1899. E. A. Ryder, a general and fancy draper, was one of the first traders in this parade. Another was G. Sorrell . . . fruiterer . . . 'families waited on daily'. Several of the shops have yet to be let and the builders appear to have only just finished decorating at the Post Office.

A day by the sea. The Southend Corridor Express with two District Railway electric locomotives leaving Ealing Broadway. The service began on 1 June 1910 and lasted until 1 October 1939. Steam locomotives were in charge of the trains from Barking. The carriages were owned by the London, Tilbury & Southend Railway. Even in London Transport days there was a lot of advertising for this service and there were special rates for large parties. For example, from Hounslow Town to Southend (via Acton Town), the return fare was 4s 4d (21½p).

Pinner. Paines Lane about 1914, with early Metro-land houses. The lane still keeps much of its rural features to this day. Many of these early outer Metro-land developments managed to retain something of the countryside spirit that later developments consistently failed to do.

Clapham Road Underground Station. The old station on the City & South London Railway, 1914, now Clapham North.

2

NORTHERN HEIGHTS

The Underground extensions to Cockfosters, Barnet & Edgware.

The country north of London was as rural as west Middlesex at the turn of the century. It was served by the lackadaisical steam rail services of the Great Northern Railway, by electric trams, and later by the expanding and aggressive bus services.

In the Barnet area, a local horse-drawn cab service, run by a Mr Parsloe, easily dealt with local traffic from New Barnet station to the little town, surrounded as it was by fields and hedgerows almost to the horizon. Some development had taken place around the town, and this gradually spread along the ribbon of land beside the main roads linking to London. But away to the east, the country consisted of a number of quite large estates including the estate known as Bohun Lodge, and Osridge, owned by Sir Thomas Lipton, the Victorian tea magnate, which together with Oak Hill Park and Monkfrith, made a solid slab of private green amid the farmlands between East Barnet and Southgate villages.

The Piccadilly Line of the Underground, that was to open up this area in the 1930s, had had its eastern terminus at Finsbury Park since 1906. The Great Northern Railway, which owned and had built Finsbury Park station, viewed the Underground Line as nothing other than a feeder for its own services to Barnet, Hatfield and Welwyn. However, other plans had formulated inside the brain of an American Banker, John Pierpoint Morgan, who as early as 1902 had formed a syndicate to build new Tube railways, including a line from Hammersmith out to Southgate, then little more than a huddle of cottages, a smithy, a church and chapel. A rival scheme, promoted by his co-patriot Yerkes and the London United Tramways, was also concerned with building a line from Hammersmith, and these people naturally had opposed the Morgan scheme. Parliament at that time found that the Morgan Bill no longer represented the scheme which the House had

provisionally sanctioned, so the Morgan scheme, in its original form, was withdrawn.

For Barnet, Underground rail services were to prove very slow in coming; in fact it was only during the second World War that the old main lines were electrified for electric working. But until something could be agreed about the Finsbury Park problem the north London proposals towards Southgate were also 'in the air' and could well have ended up with the same timescale as Barnet. Under an Act of August 1902, the proposals north of Finsbury Park were abandoned and the company, now the Great Northern, Piccadilly & Brompton Railway, went ahead with work in the west of London. Unfortunately, with the abandonment of powers an agreement with the Great Northern, under which future extensions north of Finsbury Park would not be carried out without Great Northern consent, became operative; also no 'through' trains could be run on such a line if it were built, nor could such a line be leased to outside controlling parties.

This state of affairs was to help keep down north London expansion; although naturalists chasing butterflies over Hampstead Heath in 1910 were able to note, in a record of these ambulations, that the glint of villa roofs was catching the sun in their march across much of the green distance. The spread of London suburbia was assisted, at the same time, by some long-running tramway routes, with the London County Council gaining powers to run over the Metropolitan Electric Tramways to North Finchley and Barnet.

However, by the end of the first World War, the public clamour for something to be done about the bad travelling conditions for the new London commuters began to gather momentum. It was no good having a home if it could not be reached easily after work, and enjoyed. And, of course, the working hours in those days were very extended so that the travel problems, which became increasingly abundant, could not be eased away by the staggering of working times.

The press of those days, as indeed today, saw good reporting material in this popular daily misery of movement. The *Daily Mirror* press campaign at the end of 1922 certainly directed the public outcry for such an extension of the Underground Line from Finsbury Park, and the Minister concerned had to face a large number of public deputations from the Finsbury Park area, each having the same tale of distress to tell as workers fought to board trams and buses for their homes. Men and women, it was said, had to fight in rugby-type scrums for a place on the vehicles. And whilst this was going on, pickpockets fell upon the unfortunate people. Working with a skill that could be likened to that of the present day, the agitators sought the help of doctors to describe the nervous conditons that seemed to strike at the prettiest women, whilst others spoke of the diseases of the chest that took many a man, who had survived the trenches of Flanders, quickly into his grave.

However, when an MP was able to say that he had been knocked down himself whilst attempting to board a tram at Finsbury Park, Parliament stirred itself more effectively than it had done especially when faced with a high-powered petition of some 30,000 signatures. This was presented in June 1923, after it had become known that the Underground Group had gone into south London because of the obstruction of the London & North Eastern Railway, based on the long-lamented agreement which was made with its predecessor. A Public Enquiry was called for.

The Report, which appeared on 17 March 1926, took a clear course for action to be taken – a train service from north and north-west London into the West End. It also suggested that an extension of the Underground was an obvious step. As a matter of urgency, the Piccadilly Line should be extended to Manor House; also, the Report went on, a further extension made towards Wood Green and, if possible, even to Southgate.

Witnesses to the committee had suggested that there was no cause to fear competition between main line trains of the LNER and new Underground trains, as the main line had the advantage of higher speeds to attract traffic from areas further away from London. Also, it was planned to take the Underground extension away from the line of route of the main line. In this way, the Underground, when it did arrive, struck through acres of fields to Cockfosters, which was nowhere in particular.

The London & North Eastern had generally neglected its suburban lines for decades, a practice that had gained momentum during the war years. Those passengers who were forced to use its trains complained of their being irregular, and letters to the press spoke often of the poor standard of service. The report, therefore, was welcomed generally, none more so than by a number of astute estate agents and developers who had already smelt big profits for the taking, after pleasant experiences in the Hendon and Finchley areas before the first World War.

However, there was the usual delay when it came to discovering who was to pay for such a laudible scheme. It was not until the summer of 1929, in fact, with the Government of Ramsay MacDonald and his Labour Party that the Development (Loan Guarantees and Grants) Bill was published, so enabling the loan capital at last to be raised for the Piccadilly Line extension in north and west London. The extension to Southgate was the single biggest item qualifying for grant. There was every hope that there would be no further opposition from the LNER; however, this was soon to be shattered when Sir Ralph Wedgwood, for the main line company, opposed the proposals for the Southgate extension, on the ground that it considered there would be a loss of some £100,000 a year through the reduction of interchange passengers flowing through Finsbury Park. The Company was alarmed at the way things had gone, and proposed that it should electrify its own line to Welwyn, with branches serving High Barnet and Edgware.

The Bill, however, was not stopped, for this was a time when attempts were being made to deal with London's transport needs from a global and comprehensive viewpoint, so reducing the 'pirates' on the road, and paving the way for the formation of the London Passenger Transport Board only a few years later.

During the building of the extension from Finsbury Park there was much local pressure (common when a new Tube is built) for a *local* station, and especially the distance of about 1½ miles between Manor House and Turnpike Lane was raised, with a request for an intermediate station. Frank Pick, the Underground's Vice-Chairman and main promoter of the scheme, refused this. In his view any station should serve as an interchange for bus and tram routes; but between these two stations the trains would run parallel with road services and he saw no point in a station which would have little interchange possibilities. With the success of work in south London to Morden, which was already to earn money and praise, the land developers could only watch with joy at the opportunity opening up in north London.

The Underground stations were given great planning care, with Pick taking a very direct and central role. He was able to write to his Chief Engineer about Bounds Green, completed in Spring 1933 (although it had been open for the previous eight months): 'I am pleased with Turnpike Lane station now it is completed. The subways are an improvement on [those] previously built. Altogether we have . . . a credit to our undertaking.'

It was, of course, at the far ends of the new line that land was cheapest, and where developers and new house buyers had much to gain. The Great Depression had hardly lifted, yet the misery did bring cheap labour, and in London a gradually increasing optimism had promoted the feeling of a great new age. It gave everyone just a hint of intoxication after the dreary reminders of the horrors of war. In north London, as elsewhere

around the capital, the message was the same – get out to the fields and bird-song! It was missing the point for a columnist of the *Palmers Green and Southgate Gazette* to pontificate: 'The young married couple of today prefers a small flat more to their taste, and are loath to burden themselves with a large house. I visited a new home of two young friends the other day and was amazed to see how comfortable and spacious only two rooms can be if they have been cleverly furnished.' Most Londoners had had enough of rooms, and the prospect of a new house, at little more than the rent for two rooms nearer town, meant that the estate developers had no great selling problems, other than over-supply, by the mid-Thirties.

The construction of the Tube railway was able to move apace when the area round the new Arnos Grove station was reached, for the new line was then to run on the surface through rural country. Trees were cut, hedges felled, and the rattle of contractors' wagons brought such an air of excitement that the prim local council was prepared to look with affability at the planning requests that arrived for further housing projects.

In 1933, before the proposed date for the opening of the extension from Arnos Grove to Enfield in mid-March, there were houses going up at The Birches, directly overlooking Oakwood Park, for £1,115 freehold – a considerable sum for those days, and an indication of the high-class type of housing which was allowed. Part of the Lipton Estate went up for sale in that year, but all thoughts were on the new railway.

When the Enfield West and Southgate sections opened on 13 March 1933, public excitement reached fever pitch. The air was heady with talk of the new London Passenger Transport Board which was planned to take over in the following July, and the 'brave new world' image infected everyone. The railway, it was reported, on Opening Day had issued 30,000 free tickets for use after 10am and all but a few had been used. There were special facilities for the people of Hounslow and district to visit the new extension from Arnos Grove to Enfield West, and throughout the day there were packed trains arriving from the west.

There had been many of the same opinion as a letter-writer in the local press who had complained, during the previous month, of the deplorable conditions in the LNER suburban services in these terms:

Sir, I wonder whether the governing board of the suburban services of the LNER will look into the travelling conditions that regular passengers and season tickets holders experience daily. The dirt on the carriages is common knowledge, but until recently there had been some effort to keep them clean, at least for 1st class passengers. Now they are uncomfortable and cold. I instance the 9.19, with a change at Finsbury Park into a Moorgate train that is even colder still. There are many who say that the quicker the whole of the railway becomes another branch of the Tube, the better it will be for all of us.

The press and media generally vied with each other for descriptive intoxication. Someone had said that the site of the new Enfield West station was the highest point in Europe, if a straight line were drawn, until the Urals were reached. When challenged on this, the newspaper said that it was given this information by 'one of the Underground engineers at the site'. The publicity authorities of the Underground were quick to challenge this; Mr Duncan, the Officer concerned, stating with dry humour: 'I believe that you will find it is Cockfosters and not Enfield West that is the highest point, although I am not sure that I could take the risk of such a journey to verify this, as the course would pass over miles of sea, including the Kiel Canal and the Gulf of Riga.'

The exhilaration of the new Underground seemed to captivate the very old as well as the young marrieds looking for their dream house – one old lady, a Miss Mary Brown, had said openly that she had never ridden on a tram or a bus but, when interviewed just before the opening of Southgate station, said that her last wish would be to see the great new architectural wonder before she was 'taken'. Happily, this wish was granted when she was pushed in a bathchair by some young cub reporters to the station and was also shown some of the new houses being built nearby. She died a short time afterwards with a happy smile.

Yet though most locals welcomed the stirring change of the railway in the Southgate and west Enfield areas, some old diehards clung to their vanishing way of life. One such old lady, who was on her way to attaining 100 years of age at this time, said the secret of long life was entirely due to the fact that she had gone unwashed for 80 years! Newcomers to the Southgate area, with its 'way of health' and its spick-and-span new black-and-white dadoed bathrooms, quite naturally recoiled in horror at such a heresy. Perhaps too much sex or no drinking, but not washing – how frightfully dreadful! 'We Southgate people in our new houses are a pretty clean and gentlemanly lot. We don't boast about our baths and bathrooms, but the fact remains that we take our ablutions seriously,' somebody growled.

Residents found that the new services of bus and train serving Enfield West station were very convenient as a rapid means of travel to business, and many people used the curtailed 629 service to reach the station. By the end of April 1934, the news came out that the new transport authority had considered the name of the Enfield West station, following local moves, and had decided to avoid any confusion by adding in brackets after the name of Enfield West the word 'Oakwood'. Residents were assured that in a very short time this new name would be a regular district name for the area.

And, sure enough, the new district was not long in getting established. There had been a limited development in the area during the early 1920s, but nothing to the mass of bricks and mortar that started to flow over the open fields with the coming of the Tube. The position of Enfield West station was for some months in the middle of 'wide open spaces' and as the roads for the new houses cut through hedges and fields, the local big estates were being swept away. Thirty London firms were developing the Southgate Estate in 1934, with the Davies-built Hampden Way Estate houses going for £695. The Ideal Housing Company, also at work, strove to sell its dearer houses with the advertisement that was 'inserted to catch the eye of prospective purchasers who are willing to purchase a house of £1,000'.

Local Town Planning attempted to control the spread of housing in an ordered way 'to preserve health and the amenities, as more and more people are choosing Southgate for the first time, where the land offers so much that is still blissful and remote'. But it was to be remote for only a very short time as the housing ('no cheap and nasty project allowed') swept out from the stations. In Southgate at this time there were already 1,000 houses and by 1935 the punch-drunk public were told that there would be double that amount. Few voices were raised for the preservation of rural life – all was in the name of Progress. As one writer in the area put it in 1934:

Taking a stroll in the direction one is amazed at the progress made. Rural life has ceased at the hands of the builder; pleasant walks have been replaced by trim roads, many of which have not yet been completed. The old stile by Osidge Lane stands as a pathetic reminder of lost days. One wonders how many troths were plighted there. The axeman has got to work with his axe, and the sound and snort of mechanical excavators in Osidge Lane make it a shadow of its former self.

But nobody gave a second look at the heap of smashed timber that represented the ancient stile, or the way of life it marked. We were in the 1930s; the modern age of talkies and of Amy Morrison (neé Johnson). Hendon, the cradle of flying, was only down the road – so 'why not provide, in these golden 1930s days, for a *local* aerodrome for Southgate, before all the land is built over?', a Councillor was heard to ask.

This heady excursion into the future was too much for the Southgate and Enfield locals. One man asked in boldest rhetoric: 'Will this proposition for an aerodrome bring more peace and quiet to this area? Only a small proportion of people actually work here; practically all go to the City. One of the main attractions of an aerodrome is to reach *other* places more quickly, but those who live in the Southgate area do not want to go to other places, but to live quietly at home.' It was striking a chord; there was, after all, excitement enough with new homes and new gardens, and for entertainment, just down the road, the new cinemas bringing Hollywood escapism into everyone's lives.

In the Spring of 1934, English films were competing with the best of Hollywood, but going the rounds was that rollicking account of England's past – *The Private Lives of Henry VIII* – with a much-loved and rising English actor, Charles Laughton, to remind everyone about the Englishman's home being his castle.

The Osidge Lane development, announced in 1934, was touched with a certain amount of romantic grandeur, for the estate was the brainchild of a 29-year-old young man called Hugh Davies who had worked his way up the estate manager's profession just at the right time, founding his own estate agent's business in Southgate in December 1933, employing a staff of three people. He had worked for seven years previously with the established firm of P.H. Edwards, operating in Golders Green, Kenton and Mill Hill. Hugh Davies also created London & Suburban Homesteads Ltd to develop the land in this area; by the start of the war, he employed some 400 staff in north and south London.

His Osidge Lane development was large – over one million pounds was involved with the purchase of this large slice of land around Sir Thomas Lipton's mansion of Osidge, just 'up the

road' from the new Southgate station. Care was taken to give a sense of spaciousness to the web of residential roads that sprung up here, and to make sure that, with few exceptions, the roads did not lead directly through the area so that the blissful traffic-free nature of life, which had existed hitherto around Osidge Lane, could be allowed to continue as far as practicable.

But, as always where money can be made, things moved too fast for such comfort. More and more people, many carrying their copy of the *Evening Standard's* 'Guide to House Purchase', were on their way out to Southgate and to Cockfosters, making the clamour for land louder and more insistent. The 'Guide' gave helpful hints on everything from the servant problem to roof coverings and boundaries, from mortgages to drains. 'Don't become alarmed if cracks appear in your ceiling,' the book said, soothingly; adding that 'the wise householder will endeavour to trace the water supply from stop valve to storage tank' – a hint that proved only too well-timed in those days of lead pipes and winter freezes in unlagged roofs.

And so, during the rest of the 1930s, the Cockfosters extension of the Piccadilly Line saw the remorseless removal of the surviving landed estates and parks. Two years after the Osridge development, there came, in 1936, the sale of the Monkfrith Estate land just to the north of it. It was advertised as '50 acres of really major building land at a time when there is very little land for building purposes in the district'. This sale was followed, inevitably, the following year by the sale of the adjacent estate, that of Bohum Lodge, an oddly-shaped piece of property just south of Cat Hill, and closer to Cockfosters than Southgate. It realised some £75,000, a very large sum for those times. Here it was planned to build at 8 houses to the acre.

In 1938 a surviving piece of land known as Oakwood Park, near Southgate station, provided more houses whilst, in the same year, the Southgate Estate of Messrs

Laing offered houses of high standard and very contemporary design from around £1,140 – almost double the price of the houses on lesser developments in London. There was, with Laing, the luxury of fitted kitchens; although 'compact' there were folding seats and a put-away ironing board; and leaded lights at the windows. On Laing's Southgate North Estate, claimed in a flush of exuberance to be the 'most beautiful estate in north London', the Jubilee House went at £995, whilst the 'Coronation' type, with its prominent Odeon-like rounded entrance front, was priced at £1,140. The estate went up some three minutes' walk from Southgate and close to the open land of Trent Park.

All around the new houses of Arnos Grove, Southgate, Cockfosters and Barnet was the promise of convenience – schools, trains 'about every minute' to Town, picnics, golf courses, easy shopping and, of course, cinemas and dance halls, for such places were the temples of health and happiness in the 1930s. There was even a strong accent on 'gym', in line with what was happening on the Continent, especially in Greater Germany at the time. We may suppose that 'gym' was to the 'with it' and weight-conscious girl of those days, what Yoga is to their granddaughters today. Certainly there are indications that the sight of these beauties at exercises delighted many of the new breed of Southgate male. In the newspapers of the time one man wrote: 'Girls, take advice from a man, especially if you want to dance! Mr Singer of the Junior Ladies of Bowes Park and District invites you to roll along and support us in numbers. I can confidently state that young ladies do really need the benefit of physical exercise! They do not know just how attractive they can look when giving a display of their proficiencies. Girls who happen to be awkward or heavy in their gait will improve by deportment. Finally, young girls who are intending to go dancing will find the course of gymnastics of immense value in this pastime, where lightness of foot is essential.'

The Edgware extension. In the early 1920s, the plans for extending the Hampstead Tube from Golders Green were revived. Despite some houses having been built over the projected route at Golders Green, parcels of land further north had already been acquired and fenced by 1913. Much additional expense was, however, incurred with the need to purchase the houses and land at Golders Green and demolish the houses to make way for the viaduct which was to carry the Underground. In order to save compensation money, sometimes only half a semi-detached house was bought, the other half remaining very close to the trains. The extension also included some heavy engineering work just north of Hendon Station.

The old village of Hendon stands on a hill called the Burroughs and the new line was carried beneath by twin tube tunnels, more than half-a-mile long.

The LNER terminus at Edgware offered a poor train service to London via Finchley, although there was a fairly busy goods and coal yard. The yard lasted long after the last steam train (1941) and was not closed down and the track removed until 4 April 1964. The LNER route was to have formed the Northern Line extension from Finchley via Mill Hill, which was never finally completed.

The Hampstead Tube station at Edgware was designed in a classical Italian style by S. A. Heaps, and was 'sufficiently dignified to command respect'. There were intermediate stations between Golders Green and Edgware at Brent (originally to have been named Woodstock), Hendon Central, Colindale and Burnt Oak, each having 150ft-long island platforms. At Edgware a bus station was laid out in the forecourt. Provision was also made for a further extension into Hertfordshire – Watford was at one time proposed. The shops opposite the station were built on deep concrete walls strong enough to form the sides of a short tunnel.

The line opened as far as Hendon on 19 November 1923, when the ceremony was performed by the President of the Board of Trade, Sir Philip Lloyd Grahame MP, who was at that time the Hendon MP. The Edgware section opened on Monday, 18 August 1924. But Burnt Oak station remained unopened until 17 October due to labour troubles. Some of the other stations lacked final architectural details for a few weeks.

Passing loops were later provided at Hendon and Brent to enable non-stop trains to be run at peak periods, from 13 February 1927 until 22 August 1936. The extension was a great success. The smart new trains in Post-Office red, with white upper panels and chocolate waistbands, were soon filled with people not only from the districts along the line, but from places further afield. Often the feeder bus services brought them from quite some distance to Edgware. Here they could board one of the frequent trains and be in Charing Cross and the Tottenham Court Road in 35 minutes. The LNER steam trains from Edgware took 58 minutes to reach King's Cross.

Commenting on the opening, *The Times* of 17 March 1923 stated: 'The hitherto quiet and purely rural Edgware village is seeing a new and steadily rising level of land values . . . the district presents plenty of opportunities.'

Opportunities, indeed, for the land agents and builders! One of the first on the scene at Edgware was George Cross. He bought seventy acres in October 1919 and made a handsome profit when part of this land was purchased by the Underground Group for the site of the station and sidings.

Cross was later instrumental in creating the modern Edgware, and many years later he was to recall the thrill he got in helping to build a new district: 'In moulding that slice of the suburbs of London in any way I pleased; planning roads as I would; naming them as I fancied.'

Those were the days when planning laws were simple and local councils seldom intervened.

One of the earliest large-scale developments was at Burnt Oak, where the London County Council laid out a vast estate from 1926.

By 1925 Hendon and Edgware were spreading over the hills and fields at a speed that amazed visitors. One writer in a feature on new houses around London wrote: 'Within the last two or three years a considerable change has taken place, and a beautiful garden suburb has sprung up at Edgware. Handsome shops are already erected, and good wide roads have been constructed, or are in course of construction.'

Soon the London newspapers were bristling with advertisements for houses alongside the new railway. H. Sousley announced his Deans Lane Estate, Edgware, by encouraging inner suburban dwellers to come out to Edgware's green fields with his slogan 'No More Landlords'. But he was selective when it came to the people he wanted on his estates: 'Strictly satisfactory references required . . . weekly repayment 35/- [£1.75p].'
The Underground posters showed a row of Victorian terraced houses and the headlines: 'Leave this and move to Edgware.' Later posters asked: 'Edgware . . . live there. Live where? Edgware!'

Soon the newspapers were full of advertisements for Haymills Estates at Hendon, with architecturally-designed houses by Herbert Welch. 'Hendon is one of the prettiest of the residential places to live . . . and for residential purposes it is enhanced by a first class railway service.'

At Golders Green, there was still plenty of land for new houses: 'Many house hunters who have not yet visited Golders Green will often have heard its name mentioned in connection with the garden city that has risen there.'

On the Empire Construction Company's Estate at Broadacre Avenue, Edgware, would-be purchasers were told that the homes were built on a site that was extremely high and that there were charming views. The developer promised that no inferior houses would spoil the area and that each house had a generous plot of land so as to avoid overcrowding.

But, as we have seen, no suburban district was considered mature until it had a cinema. In 1932 work began on the Curzon Cinema at Edgware and crowds of people watched the cranes erecting the steel framework and the bricklayers feverishly laying the walls. By 2 May 1932 the building was ready for a gala opening: 'A worthy contribution to Edgware,' said the local newspaper.

Edgware station yard was also provided with shops and a large neo-Tudor pub with elaborate plasterwork that reminded one of Liberty's department store in London.

Soon the multiple shops spread along the parades – Woolworths, Sainsburys, Montague Burtons and small shops of every kind. Edgware was virtually complete by the mid-1930s and Frank Pick and Lord Ashfield were already thinking of those virgin green fields of Hertfordshire, just north of Edgware terminus. The Northern Line to Elstree featured in their 1935–6 New Works plans, but it was a dream that was never to be fulfilled.

High Barnet. Bus-train link of the 1890s. This is Parsloe's horse-bus service waiting for the afternoon train, about 1900. Mr Parsloe ran a horse-taxi service that was a familiar sight around the Barnet streets. He advertised that he met 'Trains from Barnet station, at Metropolitan fares'. His service ran, in the mornings, from Barnet at 8.20am, leaving High Barnet at 8.35am and arriving at New Barnet Station at 8.50am. From the lack of accommodation in this little vehicle, it is clear that the taxi service did not attract many local passengers.

High Barnet. Local train, with a freight train beyond. The milk churn, to be seen in the luggage van, is an indication of the considerable amount of milk still being supplied by regions close to London for use in the City. There was much milk trade from Hertfordshire and Buckinghamshire at the turn of the century, and the Metropolitan Railway ran special milk vans up to Finchley Road daily for this trade.

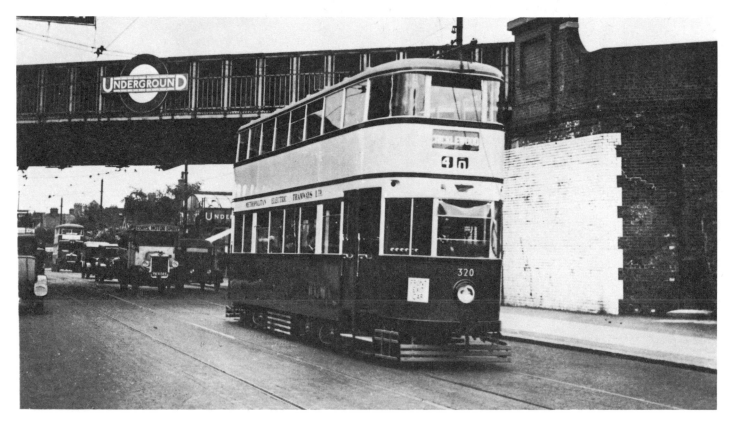

Golders Green. A Metropolitan Electric Tram, route 40, under the Hampstead Tube bridge in the early 1930s. Car 320 was built by the Union Construction and Finance Co in 1929 as one of a series of experimental trams incorporating the latest equipment and designs. The car had a short life, being scrapped in 1936.

Just under the bridge is the canopy to the station – a facility erected on 18 December 1911 to provide cover for the transfer of tram to tube passengers.

Barnet. The early years. Unmade roads and an occasional lamp greet the milk roundsman.

Golders Green. Golders Green in 1927. By this time, in under a decade, the place is surrounded by the paraphernalia of the post-war world – shops, houses, banks, and war memorials. Motor cabs wait in ordered lines, and the bus station, an early example of interchange, is filled with open-top 'NS', 'K', and 'S' buses.

Barnet. An early tram at Barnet, bound for Highgate. One local resident recalled: 'For us children, the excitement of a tram-ride made the week, and it really did seem that we were in the 20th century, as we sped from Barnet, perched high up upon the wooden seats of the upper deck and staring down on the lesser folk below.'

Barnet. This old photograph records a triumphant local event – the departure of the first electric tram from Barnet to Highgate. The service was to bring the local people within easy reach of London by road, avoiding the indifferent local train service at that time. The tram, with 'Special' showing, seems to contain Operating dignitaries, including the Superintendent (in bowler hat) and some worried electricians who stare upwards towards the overhead wires.

Mill Hill. Not reached by Underground trains until as late as 1941, it has arguably been least affected by the rash of modern housing. This country lane is Daws Lane, now filled with houses which have retained some of this lost character.

One resident recalls: 'Of all the land between Pittacy Hill and the railway, hardly a road was built over. Wild life of all kinds was to be seen there and from the Midland Railway an almost unbroken line of country stretched to Edgware Road and Orange Hill, past the 'Green Man', with a few cottages almost the only habitations within reach.'

Turnpike Lane. The extension of the Piccadilly Line to Southgate was carried out with monies granted under the Development (loan guarantees and grants) Act of 1929 for the relief of unemployment. Certainly this scene at Turnpike Lane site shows plenty of work going on! A St Mary's Wharf steam-fired wagon, a customary heavy lorry of the time, hurries away on its solid tyres with a roar of steam.

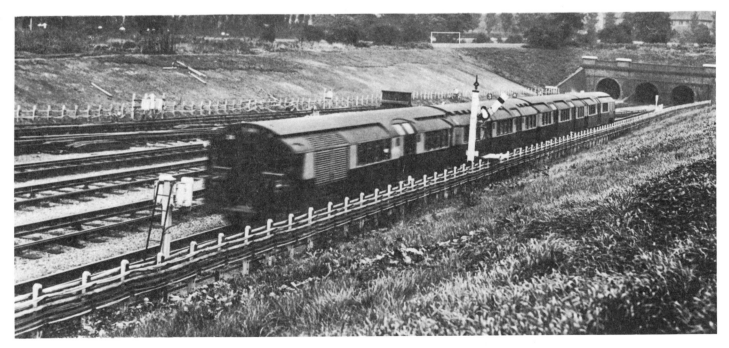

Golders Green. Train composed of 'Standard' stock cars emerges into the daylight after its long journey under London. The tracks on the left lead to Golders Green depot.

Hendon. The 'Greyhound' inn at Church End, Hendon, about 1903; a hostelry which was severely damaged in 1676, and has been several times rebuilt since the 17th century. First mentioned in a Parish minute book of 1655, it was formerly known as the Church House, being built on church property. The rent for this was used to reduce the Poor Rate. The inn actually issued its own coins with the legend 'Hendon, value one halfpenny'. Like the coin, this scene has long since been swept away by modernisation.

Edgware. Village street c1909, as Car 74 of the Metropolitan Tramways is preparing to leave for London. Edgware village was a popular place for tram excursionists. Teas were available at 'popular prices' near the tram stop. The more adventurous, having seen the old church and the legendary forge said to have inspired Handel's 'Harmonious Blacksmith', could go on to rural Canons Corner and visit The Corner House tea gardens, where there was room for a hundred people.

Hendon. How the local doctor made his rounds: this ancient print shows a doctor's horse and cart coming up Parsons Street, Hendon, near the present crossing, the Great North Way. The time is about 1880.

Colindale, 1923. The Edgware extension: A steam-powered mechanical excavator at work filling a little train of contractor's wagons with spoil. Boundary fencing is already in place. The excavator was owned by The Foundation Company.

Colindale. Another of the contractor's trains on the Edgware extension, at the embankment near Colindale. This locomotive possesses a covered cabin; contrast with the previous photograph.

Edgware. Oh, the excitement and wonder of it all! Edgware station is open at last, with its pretty gabled roofs and clever bus interchange. This was the scene in April 1927, with a mass of activity as school parties prepare to board a 142 bus waiting in the courtyard, rich motorists await the arrival of friends hoping to buy a new house in the district, and new arrivals seek to find their way to the estates.

Sham-Gothic. An up-market approach by Curton, building near Edgware Underground station. This unusual approach suggested that the happy buyer could have what amounted to a small baronial hall in his home, with sham timbers and Gothic-style brick fireplace. These were, of course, very expensive homes.

Southgate. Southgate station shortly after the second World War. There is still an air of the country about this important interchange station which was so interesting when first erected that it made a major attraction for elderly established residents who were more used to horse-and-cart days.

50

Southgate station, with its integral bus station, in April 1984.

Interior of standard stock. Passengers on the Piccadilly Line extensions made their journeys in Tube cars like this, the last word in seating, lighting and comfort in 1930. This picture was taken in 1935 and the advertisements are of interest. Cossor Radio sets; an appeal by LPTB for staggered working hours; the magazine *Everybody's* that few suburban homes were without until the rival *Picture Post* began in 1938; and Senior's meat and fish pastes for those lace-like sandwiches that were made specially for Aunt Lucy's mid-week visit.

Much of the seat upholstery was designed by Enid Marx or Marian Dorn for Frank Pick, with fabric woven by John Holesworth & Co Ltd of Halifax.

Wood Green. One of the new Piccadilly Line stations: Wood Green in April 1935. Interchange between the new Tube lines and road transport was a main plank in Pick's policies at the time. Here city commuters hurry from the 39A tram, their hands prepared to reach into pockets for their season tickets. The monthly season ticket was always being pushed by publicity, as it cut down queues and sped passenger movement in the rush hours.

Wood Green. An evening rush hour scene at Wood Green in March 1938. At this time the contrast between the Victorian stations and the spacious, well-lit entrances to the new Underground stations must have been greatest. These people would have worked in City Offices, for very few London stores closed until late evening.

Steam at Edgware: The old village terminus with an LNER train on 5 June 1937.   [H. C. Casserley]

Modern temple: the cinema. At 3pm on Monday, 24 March 1934, the Gaumont Palace at Wood Green was open for the first time to the eager public. The opening ceremony of this new *Art-Deco* palace was performed by the Mayor of Wood Green. This artist's impression of the new cinema, one of many opened that year throughout the London area, comes complete with the film titles. And there is the promise of a lovely cup of tea afterwards in the cafe/restaurant!

Southgate. Semi-detached houses nearing completion in Raith Avenue. Leaded lights and brick boundary walls are in position, although no attention has yet been given to public verges. All the building employees were usually on piece-work, and the houses were 'rushed along', with shells being fitted out as soon as the main structure was complete.

Arnos Grove. The London and Suburban Homesteads Group was one of several building groups active in the Southgate and Arnos Grove area in the 1930s. This mid-Thirties scene shows staggered 'semis', in course of erection. This building firm was part of the Hugh Davies organisation and was to expand rapidly just before the second World War.

Arnos Grove. Another contemporary photograph on the Arnos Grove
Estate, when Morton Way had just been completed.

Southgate. The Whitehouse Farm Estate was another development in
the area. The choice of front enabled the new house-occupier to feel
that his house was different from his neighbours, with variations to
gables, front doors, and even exterior fencing patterns.

North London. Estate agents were anxious to stress the comparatively low weekly expense of their properties. Here the deposit was pitched quite high, for £50 was roughly half the cost of a Ford 8 saloon car, large numbers of which were starting to pour out of the factories during these years.

Southgate. Efforts by the Enfield and Southgate local authorities tended to ensure that higher-grade new housing was well represented in the district. In this old 1930s picture, semi-detached houses are on offer very competitively at below £600. They do not have garage space. Builders always tried to convey 'fringe advantages' such as 'no road charges'. These houses were erected by Harwood Nash, who called themselves 'the architectural builders', reflecting the feeling amongst many builders of the day that architects merely added unnecessarily to the cost of building.

Hendon. Looking down Greyhound Hill towards the Midland Railway arch and Aerodrome Road, about 1914. The buildings of Hendon Aerodrome can be seen in the distance, whilst on the left, by the old sign post, are the premises of the Aircraft Manufacturing Co. The Watford Way had not then been constructed. A local correspondent has recalled how in the 1900s one could still 'look across fields, thinking of generations of lovers who had walked over them, with the spire of Harrow Church in the distance, and a fair glimpse of Windsor Castle, when London fogs allowed no haze towards the south. On Bank Holidays, Mr Warner and his famous "Welsh Harp" inn beside Brent Reservoir brought down a swarm of pleasure seekers of a sort. In this delightful world away from London, corn grew high and cattle grazed on the pastures from Hinge's fields to as far as the eye could see'.

Hendon. The same spot in modern times.

Hendon. Flying days before 1914 at Hendon attracted the fashionable crowds. A Breguet biplane is crossing the finishing line. 'There can be no better place to put a car to for an afternoon than to take it to the enclosure at Hendon,' said a journal of 1914.

Hendon. In between the wars, Hendon Aerodrome became the centre for the famous RAF Pageants. (The RAF acquired the field in 1925.) Thousands flocked out by Underground to Colindale. In 1927 a fashion magazine stated: 'The King attends and in recent pageants has used wireless signals to the aeroplanes.' By then the pageant had become as much a part of the London season as Henley and Trooping the Colour.

But it was in pre-1914 days that Hendon was at its most exclusive, as these two views show. 'On Sunday afternoons Hendon is a sight for the Gods,' declared one editor.

At the 1936 pageant, a certain aircraft designer called R. J. Mitchell displayed his Spitfire 'which will be on show for the first time'. No doubt most people thought that would be the last ever heard of it. The RAF last flew from Hendon in 1957. The magnificent RAF museum is now on part of the site.

Hendon. Even before the days of the Underground at Colindale and Hendon, factories began appearing along the Edgware Road, their workers travelling by tram. About 1910 the flat fields west of Hendon began to attract a number of early aircraft manufacturing companies, who set up flight testing fields. By 1914 the main firms were the London and Provincial Aviation Co, Airco, Nieuport and General Aircraft Co, Kingsbury Aviation Co, British Caudron Co, and the most famous of all, Handley Page Ltd.

The Aircraft Manufacturing Co (Airco) built the famous DH4 designed by Geoffrey de Havilland. The company was founded by George Holt Thomas in 1912. He was an organiser of many earlier rallies and displays. This picture shows the works on the Shorelands Farm site, Edgware Road, near Stag Lane. The factory expanded on to the Grove estate by 1918 and was then employing 730,000 square feet of space and 4,400 workers, with 190 aircraft being produced monthly. Work began in 1918 at Roe Green (*top left of picture*) on a garden village for the workers. The houses had built-in cupboards, gas cookers and heating.

Hendon Central. The first building, which has already begun to reach first floor level, is to be the Westminster Bank. A nearby notice indicates that the open ground nearby will be a W. H. Smith's shop.

The rise of Hendon. The farmland that was to become Hendon overnight: open land at Hendon Central, with a bridge just in position and hardcore placed for a roundabout.

Hendon Central. The same scene ten years later. The station is now surmounted by flats and surrounded by shops. The roundabout saw little heavy traffic by today's standards. An open-top 'NS' bus waits, before setting off down the new by-pass to Finchley Road and London.

The population of Hendon grew quicker than almost any other London borough. In 1921 it was 57,566. In 1931 there were 115,640 people and by 1951, 155,885.

Brent. Modern view of the station – typical of those on the Edgware extension. The spaces beside the tracks were for the passing loops used by non-stop trains between 23 June 1927 and 22 August 1936. The name suggested for this station during construction was 'Woodstock'.

Manor House. Trolleybuses formed a large part of the North London road transport network until their removal in the 1960s. In this case, the overhead wires cover a tram route. The maintenance lorries, with their ramshackle wooden tower platforms, are early marques of Armstrong, but these centre-of-the-road hazards would be unworkable in modern traffic conditions.

East Finchley. East Finchley station as it was in 1935, whilst under the control of the London & North Eastern Railway. There are two interesting period vehicles on view – a Raleigh tricycle van, and a Ford 8 Saloon which could be bought new for under £100.

Muswell Hill station in 1934. Served by the London & North Eastern Railway's suburban service, it was planned to link this branch into the Underground system before the second World War.

Woodside Park. A typical London & North Eastern suburban station: a marked contrast with the new architectural form of the stations to be found only a few miles away on the Cockfosters extension. This is Woodside Park after its takeover by the Underground. Although it is August 1953 no attempt has been made to identify it with the Underground, apart from the two 'pairs' quad-royal poster sites at the entrance.

Edgware GNR. The old Great Northern Railway terminus was situated a few yards from the terminus of the Hampstead tube of 1924. It opened as the 'temporary' terminus of the Finchley-Edgware and Watford Railway on 22 August 1867. It was to remain a terminus until its closure nearly a century later. The last passenger train steamed out in 1961 and the buildings were demolished, but freight traffic continued until 4 April 1964.

As part of the extension schemes for the Northern Line, the branch would have been used for part of its route by Tube trains from Finchley via Mill Hill East and then by way of Edgware Northern Line station to Aldenham, but only a short section was completed before the second World War. It was only because of pressure from the Government that the short section from Finchley to Mill Hill opened on 18 May 1941 to serve the barracks nearby.

3

URBAN METRO-LAND

Developments along the Metropolitan Railway. The Metropolitan Railway was the pioneer of suburban development – dating from the 19th century. Its Extension Line of the late 19th century had encouraged developments at Harrow, Pinner and Northwood. But it was the building of the branch to Uxbridge in 1904 that set the stage for the vast Metro-land developments after 1919.

The area around Wembley Park was virtually undeveloped before the British Empire Exhibition of 1924. But after the middle 1920s, housing estates began to grow along the roads and up the slopes of Barn Hill and Chalk Hill to the north of the Metropolitan Line. A Metropolitan brochure of 1927 described this area as 'one of the healthiest spots near London . . . numerous houses are already built or in course of erection. Hundreds of houses are being built in the neighbourhood, including Barn Hill, Towsend Park and Forty Lane'. Wembley Park had attracted day trippers long before the Exhibition. The story of Watkin's Tower and the early plans of the Metropolitan to make Wembley Park a rival attraction to the Eiffel Tower in Paris has been covered in our Metro-land books. After the Tower (which was never completed) was demolished in 1908, the park became a place for early flying displays and circuses. An 18-hole golf course was laid out near the site of the future Stadium (the turf was eventually used for the famous pitch). The course was popular with City men and Army officers during the first World War. There was also a golf course up on Barn Hill. Clay pigeon shooting was a popular sport at Forty Farm, the tower here being a familiar landmark for Metropolitan train passengers. The land was sold by the end of the 1920s and developed by Haymills Ltd, with houses specially designed for them by R. T. Welch, Cachemaille-Day and Lander of Lincoln's Inn. The Tudor-style houses were soon popular with film and stage people and BBC folk.

At nearby Preston hamlet were the grounds of the Uxendon Shooting Club and in 1908 the spot was chosen for the Olympic Games Shooting Contests. The Club, with the support of the twenty-seven inhabitants of the area, petitioned the Met in March 1908 for a halt to be built at Preston Lane bridge. The Met agreed to build a simple, two-platform halt on the Wembley side of the bridge, with the provision that the Club paid for half the cost. The two 260ft long platforms were opened on 21 May 1908, the first train to stop there being the 12.05 from Baker Street. Names suggested had been Uxendon and Preston Road. The bleak platform had 3ft long boards reading: 'Stop here for Uxendon Shooting School Club.'

On the opposite side of the line, beyond the bridge, was the Harrow Golf course, its distinctive club house with verandah was another local feature. In 1928 the club had 400 members. The area also had some tea rooms set in orchards.

In 1926 Preston Road was still a wayside halt where visitors alighted to see the Grove Estate. Here they could contemplate whether to buy a house from £1,025 to £1,185, 'a self-contained estate in the best part of Preston . . . only eight minutes from the station . . . carefully planned and soundly constructed houses of artistic merit and varied design, in an orchard setting of particular charm'.

Preston Road offered a palliative for 'the nerves of strained Town workers . . . a place where pure air blew in from the Chilterns!'

By 1930 a number of builders were at work, including The Bateman Building Co, Marshall's Estates and Clifford Sabey. The station was rebuilt in 1931 on the Harrow side of the bridge with the usual C. W. Clark-designed flanking shops.

By the early 1930s the houses on Barn Hill Estate were reaching up to the road between the station and Preston. At this time the whole area was busy with builders' lorries and carts (many builders still used horse transport). Everywhere were piles of bricks, blocks and sand, bags of cement and much dried mud; the smell of new paint, of wood being burnt to clear the sites; huts for the workmen, architects and site foremen, and here and there large boards proclaiming the merits of the various developments. 'On fine summer Saturdays, Preston is one of the brightest places near London. To the north there are wide spaces of attractive, open countryside.' Later, much of this area of fields was to be buried under the rapid developments that followed the opening of the Stanmore branch.

The Harrow Golf Course gave way to masses of smaller houses by the late Thirties, whilst the north side of the line was developed with high-class houses on the Woodcock Dell and Woodcock Hill Estates. The Metropolitan Railway Country Estates (MRCE) and the Metropolitan Surplus Lands Committee advertised choice sites here: 'On the site of the old Woodcock Dell Farmhouse. The large sports ground of Messrs Selfridge directly adjoins the estate, adding much to preserve the attractive features of the open countryside.'

As late as 1930, the Metro-land guide books still described the area around Harrow Hill as a place for a day trip. 'A fascinating countryside of rich pastures lies around, yet whilst encircled by rural surroundings of primitive simplicity the town is, by Metro, within 15 minutes from Baker Street.'

Uxbridge Line developments. Along the Harrow and Uxbridge branch, the post-first World War years were quiet at first. But with the sale of various country estates (notably Swakeleys at Ickenham), developments began at Ickenham and North Hillingdon in about 1922, also in the Ruislip village area. At Long Lane, Ickenham, an additional station was opened and named Hillingdon in 1923. The Swakeleys Estate was then being laid out in plots for high-class housing by Stedman and Clarke. But it was at the (then) lonely spot of Rayners Lane, where the Metropolitan had a junction with the District Railway (so bleak in winter, that the windswept platforms were known as Pneumonia Junction) that the first large-scale housing development took place. This was the Metropolitan's Harrow Garden Village Estate, which was begun in August 1929. The builder was E. S. Reid, who paid for his own sidings so that building materials could be delivered direct. The projected layout of the Garden Village was never completed. Other developers eventually moved in, but the Reid houses remained an attractive development amid oak and elm trees long after Rayners Lane ceased to be rural. One brochure persuaded Londoners to visit Harrow Garden Village, assuring them that 'on all sides of the estates were green fields and rural lanes. The air is clear and refreshing and there are upwards of 16 acres reserved for open space, tennis courts and recreation gardens'.

South of the station, the vast estate built by T. F. Nash of Harrow was started about 1931. By 1934 the firm described itself as: 'The Builder of the Future . . . over 4,000 houses constructed in the Harrow and Ruislip areas, providing homes for 14,000 people. Over 1,000 men employed.' Nash had its own joinery works at Wealdstone. The basic design was a block of six or four terraced houses, with mock Tudor facings, although later types had white walls and the imitation window shutters or curved windows in the *Art Deco* style. There were also a few semi-detached houses, and a superior-style house, with a garage, for £750.

'One word describes the Nash Estate – "satisfaction" ' said the publicity, and the London evening newspapers carried advertisements for a number of years with the headline 'From Piccadilly to the "Pic" of the houses', with an illustration of one of the Piccadilly Line experimental streamlined trains. Another advertisement for the Nash houses claimed that living at Rayners Lane would be all peace and quiet, a place 'where the din and turmoil of the streets are exchanged for an aspect of spreading landscapes . . . of trees and green pastures where the only sounds are of birds'. But it was all fantasy, for within weeks of taking up residence in your neat terraced house, with its black and white tiled bathroom and power points in every room, the next road had been completed and the footings for another road after that and so on, right the way south towards Eastcote Lane, or west to where old Field End came down from Eastcote. Nowhere was as built up as this vast estate, although the years have seen the trees, which were carefully planted in the narrow avenues, mature and provide some greenery. The only open land was a few acres reserved for allotments.

But with a home of your own for £595, and a vast array of new shops along the Alexandra Avenue leading to Rayners Lane station, people were content.

No aspect of publicity was overlooked in order to sell the estate. In about 1934 a grand shopping week was held and a temporary arch built over Alexandra Avenue. Bedecked with flags, there was a bold sign proclaiming 'Nash Homes . . . the summit of High Value'. There were firework displays and cheap evening tickets down on the Met and the Piccadilly Lines for prospective buyers. E. S. Reid also held a similar series of bonfire and firework nights on the Pinner side of the line to advertise the Harrow Garden Village Estate.

Growth was rapid: in 1930, Rayners Lane station was handling 22,000 passengers a year. By 1937 the total was a staggering four million! London Transport had to provide a temporary covered booking office and accommodation until the striking new station was opened in 1938. Its bulky towers with long windows and flanking wings was another of Charles Holden's masterpieces. The booking hall was built out over the side pavements, with ever-open sets of doors so that one had to pass through the building. The station was also at the highest point of the area and acted like a welcoming temple, either to beckon people to their daily labours in London or to tempt them to the delights of shopping and shows in the West End.

Rayners Lane was not finally to blend into Eastcote until 1940, but the development of the area around Eastcote station had begun as early as about 1912. However, it was W. A. Telling who began the modern development with houses in Morford Way soon after the war!

Parades of shops gradually replaced meadows and old cottages and the last of the famous poplar trees along Field End Road was felled. The Pavilion Teagardens were sold for development in 1935 and Laing's began their large estate. You could inspect the show houses after dark in the autumn by means of the then unique idea of floodlighting the new roads.

T. F. Nash was busy with superior-type houses east of Field End Road towards Eastcote village and Comben & Wakeling's large neo-Tudor houses were in an attractive setting at the Eastcote Park Estate, which overlooked the green meadows beside the river Pinn.

'Safeguard your dependants . . . it costs no more,' recommended the advertisements for the £1,075 houses on the Towers Estate by Howell & Burgess, off Bridle Road. Rotherham Estates and the General Housing Company were other Eastcote builders. The final completion of the shops and the unfinished estates had to wait until the 1950s.

Eastcote station was rebuilt in 1938–9 but perhaps not in such an impressive style as Rayners Lane, although the platform buildings have a lighter touch.

Ruislip Manor halt had opened in 1912 in conjunction with the Ruislip Garden City scheme. There was no development south of the railway until 1933. Then work began on another vast estate which is said to have been the largest development by any single building company at that time. Geo. M. Ball (Manor Homes) were closely associated with T. F. Nash and the design of the houses was similar. Because of the distance from the Metropolitan Railway sidings at Ruislip, a light railway system was laid down for building supplies. Some of the working areas were nearly two miles to the south near South Ruislip. Soon acre after acre of the flat, elm-lined fields were replaced by roads, crescents and closes. The main artery was Victoria Road – which took the route of the boulevard planned in the Ruislip Garden City of 1908. Parades of shops appeared south of the Ruislip Manor halt and by 1936–7 the narrow under-bridge was widened.

'Even those who feel a preference for the delights of man-made civilisation invariably find that if their days are to be spent in the big city, they are happy to return, in the quiet dusk of the evenings, to nature's stronghold outside the town,' enthused the Manor Homes Brochure. At Ruislip each house was a 'a palace in miniature' and prices started at £450 for a two-bedroomed home – with weekly repayments of 12s 2d (61p) after a £5 deposit.

'Travelling only half-an-hour from London, you will find an estate still retaining the unmarred beauties amid the unspoiled, healthy atmosphere of Nature in her most beautiful aspects.' Three-bedroomed terraced houses were £665 and there was a 'sun trap' window house for £975. Stained glass was fitted to all hall and landing windows. Each house had a kitchenette with Ideal hot water boiler (coke and coal bunkers were usually outside the kitchen window), gas-heated copper for washing clothes, draining boards in best wood and a deep kitchen sink with chromium-plated taps.

Food could be kept hygienically in a well-ventilated larder and there were kitchen cabinets and an electric ironing point. The happy housewife had the additional attractions of free light fittings throughout the house. A final touch of luxury for the 'man of small means' was a £745 house with four bedrooms. However, Ruislip-Northwood Council, although they had insisted on their rigid planning by-laws for the estate, feared that so many small houses would not produce the high rates they could have got from an estate of larger properties.

In October 1933, the Piccadilly Line trains began to run through to Uxbridge and with the increased transport facilities, the houses began to sell quickly. So rapidly did the estate grow, that Manor Homes built a public hall, but there was little provision for providing sites for churches, chapels and schools.

In 1934 a monthly season ticket on the Piccadilly Line from Ruislip to Green Park cost £1. 13s 0d (£1.65p), or by Metropolitan Railway to Baker Street £1. 14s 0d (£1.70p). The old village street had already been transformed during the 1920s into a modern shopping centre. The real seal of civilisation came in 1929, when on 3 September crowds came to the official opening of the Rivoli Cinema. A free car park and a tea lounge were additional attractions to the 1,000-seater auditorium and sound films. Later, Ruislip had a second cinema, the Astoria in High Street. South of Ruislip station, Shenley Avenue was built by H. Bowers: 'The Ruislip Station Estate . . . the estate that's different. Lose no time in paying the estate a visit, for the dream house you have yearned for is waiting to be secured at a price easily within your reach.'

Bowers offered purchasers magnificent Aztec-style fireplaces with raised hearths and well fires. The bathrooms had chromium-plated taps, pedestal basins and coloured baths. The small windows on the landings and above the main glass of the bays were coloured. The rising sun motif was a popular feature in the design. Visitors to the estate who made their way over the narrow railway bridge and down the still rural West End Road, with wooden railings painted white, saw ancient Sherley Farm on their left, then a bend in the road and they were at the estate. Here, the sales staff recommended them to call on one of the families already living there to get their unsolicited opinion on the houses before making a final decision to live on the estate.

Across West End Road, Taylor Woodrow began to fill in the fields towards the GWR main line with some roads of semi-detached bungalows. Two bedrooms, a well

fitted kitchenette and a small dining room, but most attractive of all, a large lounge, complete with a fireplace that incorporated a fitted wireless set!

At Hill Farm Estate, off Sharps Lane, buyers were told of the 'unusual and extensive views . . . of well wooded and undulating countryside'. For once, this was actually true.

'The Gem of Metro-land – each house built of all-British bricks,' went on the brochures.

Along the road to Eastcote Village and north to the Pinn valley, the Metropolitan Railway Country Estates were building houses of a style very similar to those at Harrow Garden Village. Once again, the virtues of being close to the magnificent Ruislip woods and the river Pinn were emphasised.

Ruislip High Street, as we have already mentioned, was becoming 'daily more like Ealing Broadway' – to quote a local press article. The Poplars tea gardens, famous in early Metro-land days, lay derelict and overgrown until about 1935, to be replaced by a parade of shops that included some typical household names of the period. Salmons, the ironmongers, where the smell of paraffin, cornmeal and household cleaners gave a safe and old style atmosphere to the new suburban dwellers. Then there was an ABC tea shop, the smell of fresh bread and coffee wafting across the end of Ickenham Road towards Boots the Cash Chemists and Sainsburys, where young men in high buttoned white jackets like cruise stewards, cut cheese with a wire, or patted fresh butter whilst you waited. At the end of the shop, in classical splendour of polished wood and pillars, sat the cashier.

The Scotch Wool and Hosiery Stores further down High Street, near the new Woolworths, was well stocked with wool for housewives to start their winter evening knitting. Woolworths replaced the barns and cows of Wilkins Farm, whilst the Catholic Church erected in the early 1920s was soon sold, demolished, and replaced with more shops by 1938. Lyttons department store was built on the site and just after the second World War began it opened a restaurant with potted palms, Lloyd-loom chairs and glass-topped tables.

Down near the remaining buildings of the old Ruislip (protected by a local Society) there was Williams Brothers, the north London grocers. When the shop opened in 1936 eggs were offered at 1s 3d (6p) per dozen. Thrifty shoppers quickly patronised the store, for after spending a small amount they received a thin metal token with their change. Once or twice a year, they could bring back the tokens and get cash. A similar scheme was operated by another suburban grocer chain in the Underground suburbs – Payantake Ltd.

Despite the press announcing in 1936 that Ruislip had ceased to be a holiday resort, the opening of Ruislip Lido beside the Reservoir, north of the town, on 20 May, was a grand occasion. Music, as well as 100 shapely ladies from the League of Health and Beauty, plus a cabaret in the *Art Deco* pavilion building, put Ruislip Lido on the map for water sports and as a place to take the kids to in summer.

Ickenham developed slowly, although some of the larger plots on the Swakeleys Estate were eventually sub-divided and smaller houses built by R. T. Warren.

At Ickenham work began on the Drummond estate in 1923. The builders announced that the oak trees would be preserved, as Queen Elizabeth had once picnicked beneath them! But local residents were concerned about unmade-up roads and bad drains in the village. There was also much road widening. Old Back Lane, leading to Uxbridge, was transformed in 1937 to a dual carriageway named Swakeleys Road. The old elm-lined and muddy road from Ruislip to Hillingdon was also improved out of all recognition. But there was much tree-planting with some magnificent flowering varieties.

The Ivy House Estate, with its 'unbeatable suntrap bungalows' at Hoylake Crescent, offered the young housewife of 1936 a 12ft x 10ft kitchen with 'every modern device . . . a real treasure'. Advertisements in the London papers asked: 'Getting Married? See the splendid suntrap houses and bungalows at Ickenham.'

The Ickenham Hall Estate at Milton Court on the site of Milton Farm was only partly finished before the war began in 1939. The builders, Brown & Langford had a large theatrical-style board with three-dimensional figures announcing the estate in Swakeleys Road: 'Magnificent Milton Court . . . procure while you may.'

Hillingdon village proper was over a mile from the station, which was actually on the Ickenham side of the new Western Avenue. The shopping parades at North Hillingdon grew after the Western Avenue was opened here in 1936.

A Metropolitan Railway brochure of some years before said of the new Hillingdon: 'The estate is rising on ground which till recently belonged to parkland of Hillingdon Court. The country adjoining Hillingdon station has no superior in the neighbourhood for quiet beauty and the popularity of the new suburb is already well assured.'

Hillingdon Mount Estate was 'carried out on unusual lines, affording amenities to residents not generally met with, and a large area has been reserved for tennis courts'. A house and garage on this Metropolitan estate could be yours for £5 down and £800 to pay off.

The Hillingdon Estates Company had houses for £725 upwards: 'Filled with all those conveniences so dear to the heart of the housewife. The roads are wide and there is space to ensure that purchasers have plenty of fresh air and good gardens.'

The developers of the Tudor Way Estate, off Long Lane, offered people a free lift by car from Hillingdon staton. The new shopping centre under construction would be pointed out as they sped along. 'A model Tudor Village of charming houses artistically grouped in the form of green courtyards,' they read in the brochure. There was even an impressive Tudor-style gateway, which still exists, at the entrance to the estate.

By the arrival of the A40 and the improved transport facilities, including buses to Hayes and Uxbridge, Ickenham and Ruislip, cheaper houses were being built and eventually prices for these were as low as £345. 'Britain's Wonder Houses,' read a hoarding opposite Hillingdon station. But much countryside remained and even today there are green fields between Ickenham and South Ruislip – as well as Northolt Airport.

Uxbridge has remained more of a London country town than an Underground suburb and there was really little large-scale building in the period between the wars. The clanging trams were replaced by silent trolleybuses in 1936. The old Belmont Road Station, which had waited in vain for any possible extension of the Metropolitan into Buckinghamshire, was closed and replaced by the three-track new terminus in High Street from December 1938. The design is similar to Cockfosters. There are stained-glass windows representing local heraldic devices, designed by an artist from Eastcote. The old goods yards, once so important to Uxbridge's economic life, were replaced by train sidings.

Along the Met into Hertfordshire. The Metropolitan 'Extension' Line between Harrow and Rickmansworth was finally electrified in conjunction with the new branch to Watford, on 5 January 1925. A special demonstration run was arranged for the press. The train of 'Dreadnought' steam carriages was hauled by one of the Metropolitan's famous electric locomotives, No. 20. Driver Wiggins at the controls impressed the journalists with his smooth handling and even the drinks in the Rothschild special saloon carriage, also included in the train, remained steady. Certainly, one reporter recorded: 'There is no railway undertaking in the country that has displayed more enterprise than the Metropolitan in the creation of eligible/townships residential.'

The first district the train came to after Harrow-on-the-Hill was North Harrow. By 1914, the western end of Harrow had reached out along the Pinner Road mainly by the efforts of local builder Albert Cutler. Cutler resumed operations in the Twenties and advertised extensively. In fact, Cutler was *the* builder of North Harrow! Yet, ever mindful of the main reason why people went to live in suburbs – the fresh air and the countryside close at hand – his publicity informed would-be purchasers: 'Ideal homes in North Harrow . . . for pedestrians who delight in rambles, the region might be called an enchanted ground.' So successful was the advertising, that soon North Harrow halt was proving inadequate for the new commuters and the station was rebuilt in 1929, although the wooden waiting rooms on the platforms, situated up on the railway embankment, were still rather primitive in appearance. The long gardens of the Cutler houses gave ample opportunity for gardeners and soon the district was a riot of summer roses – climbers and standards – and neat lawns. The shopping centre included branches of the banks; Cullens, the high-class grocers; the United Dairies; a wireless shop; and a chemist, where you could buy a roll of Ensign Film and, with the aid of the family box camera, try a few snaps of the children playing in the bright new garden with Spot the dog. The Headstone Hotel was an impressive, if rather gloomy, Olde English style pub by the station. It had a large hall for dances and meetings, But to make sure that everybody knew their place, there was a separate bar for workmen.

Cutler's houses eventually linked up with those of E. S. Reid and other builders at Rayners Lane, Imperial Drive being a fine new highway connecting the two places. In The Ridgeway, Cutler built his detached houses in four styles, with central heating and garages. The variety of stained-glass window designs on the Cutler estates has survived to promote a WEA study in recent years!

A. J. Pigershall was another North Harrow builder and with all this activity the 'Enchanted

Ground' eventually all but disappeared. But there was some good tree-planting and even a tiny park. By the late 1930s blocks of elegant flats with green-tiled roofs appeared along the Pinner Road. Their 'ultra-modern conveniences' included tennis courts, petrol pumps and garage, central heating, refrigerators and, in the main courtyard amid flower beds, an illuminated fountain.

Pinner's Cuckoo Hill Estate 'The City Man's Dream', was built by W. Telling of Eastcote. The detached houses were built along roads specially planted with flowering trees that over the years have made Pinner very much a green and wooded Underground suburb. The old village remained intact, except for Bridge Street. Here there was great activity in shop-building during the Thirties. The developers were very proud when they were able to tear down a picturesque Tudor farmhouse at the top of Bridge Street hill and replace it with the luxury Langham Cinema in six months. Suburbia came fast to the Middlesex countryside in those days!

But the most ambitious Metropolitan suburb along the 'Extension' Line was between Pinner and Northwood. Here there were open fields until 1930, when two businessmen, H. Peachey and Harry Neal, produced plans for a completely new suburb. A competition was held to find a name through the local press. The winner of the £5 prize was a lady from North Harrow with 'Northwood Hills'. The Ruislip-Northwood Council wasn't very impressed. It would have preferred 'Northwood Town'. Boards were erected in muddy Joel Street announcing the impending new station, which was opened in December 1933. It was the last of C. W. Clark's 'Suburban villa' style Metropolitan stations. By then London Transport was in being. Houses soon began creeping up muddy Porridge Pot Hill, which was renamed Potter Street for suburban tastes. Neal erected long parades of shops , with a W. H. Smith's newsagents, and a cinema (which in later years was known as the Rex, but started as an Odeon).

Gas was supplied by the Gas Light and Coke Co, and their steam-driven, massive delivery lorries were a familiar sight delivering coke. Power was provided by a local company, The Northwood Electric Light and Power Company.

But the first residents in the chill of winter were not completely happy. After the sophistication of inner London suburbs, they found the pioneer life had disadvantages. 'I arrived at a station,' wrote one early Metro-land pioneer, 'and stepped into mud of the most adhesive quality I had ever seen or felt . . . Yet I was to find that residing in a suburb adds a thrill and a zest to life. It is an experience in having no traditions to live up to.'

The 1934 local Ruislip-Northwood guide book rather overdid things when Northwood Hills was described as being '300ft above sea level and on the borders of Middlesex and Hertfordshire'. A cheap day ticket to take house-wives to Baker Street on one of the smart compartment-type electric trains cost 1s 7d (8p) return.

Northwood had, of course, been the first suburb last century on the Metropolitan main line. The Gatehill Estate was built during the years between the two world wars, but much of the area remained wooded or covered by golf courses.

Lord Levershulme purchased historic Moor Park after the war and it was through his Unilever Property Company that the grounds were developed as the famous golf course, also for a highly exclusive housing development. The architecturally-designed houses on their huge plots were advertised as 'combining the facilities of London with rural amenities'; each house was built to individual requirements and had 'every device for comfort and convenience'. Long drives, shrubberies, and many trees screened the tennis courts and terraces (or what we now call patios) from passing stares; but passers-by, unless they were going to the wooden station of Moor Park & Sandy Lodge, were discouraged by gated approach roads. At Moor Park, City men could live a life of luxury 'in the grounds of an historic old English Park' and yet be within forty minutes of Baker Street by fast electric expresses.

Moor Park & Sandy Lodge was the junction for the Watford branch line. It was the immediate post-first World War period which saw a number of branch line schemes before the Metropolitan Board. One plan was a Harefield and Chalfont Line, which would have branched from the Harrow and Uxbridge near Eastcote and run along the Pinn River valley through the edge of Ruislip Woods. A Local Development and Light Railway Company was formed and approached the Ministry of Transport for a Light Railway order on 10 February 1922. Robert Selbie, the Met's progressive General Manager, thought that the line would 'open an attractive residential area'. The Metropolitan proposed contributing £90,753 towards construction. But nothing ever came of this scheme.

Another scheme was the Misbourne Valley branch – once again branching from Eastcote and going through Ruislip to the Colne and then the Misbourne Valley to the Chalfont country. But the heavy engineering works that would have been involved proved the end of that scheme.

Eventually, the Met resurrected its pre-1914 plan to reach Watford High Street. Indeed, a building had actually been erected in High Street and was in use as a restaurant. But the land behind, required for the tracks, was never purchased. No doubt the citizens of Watford, which was at that time already being spoiled by industry, would have objected strongly to the Met's plan to carry the branch over Cassiobury Park by a low viaduct.

The line was eventually built with a terminus at the edge of Cassiobury Park. The house had recently been pulled down and the parklands partly preserved, the remainder to be developed for good-class housing. The new terminus and Croxley station were in C. W. Clark's usual suburban villa style

and had generous platforms, and at Watford a vast freight yard. For the Met saw Watford as a potential area to increase its freight traffic.

At the opening lunch at Oddfellows Hall, Watford, October 1925, Selbie was enthusiastic and told the pressmen: 'Tonight we finish with the traffic from Wembley Park Exhibition and on Monday we prepare to deal with the crowds from Watford.'

The booking offices at Croxley and Watford were opened in advance so that information and season tickets could be sold. Advertisements in the papers depicted the Watford station building thronged with vast crowds: 'Travel by the new route . . . easiest and best.' But although the lavish passenger and goods services were run jointly with the LNER, the latter company was not very enthusiastic, and after the General Strike of 1926, the Marylebone steam trains ceased for ever from Watford. The terminus was so far from Watford town that the Met ran its own bus services, connecting with every train.

But the builders soon got to work at Croxley. In 1931 *Metro-land* described the area: 'Croxley bids fair to grow rapidly. Till lately it was somewhat difficult of access; its inhabitants are now offered almost a superabundance of transport facilities.' But the suburb was not built up very much before 1939 and even now is bordered by some attractive country.

Cassiobury Park, Watford, was the place 'To be Healthy and Happy . . . come and live in Watford,' said the advertisements of J. Randall. 'Ideal homes and charming unspoilt country,' said E. W. Puddifoot, whose houses were fitted with the Watford Minor wrought steel boiler: 'The very latest and most efficient boiler made for domestic hot water supplies.'

Cassiobury was well developed: 'It is to the development of such carefully planned housing such as at Cassiobury that the historians and sociologists of the future will point when identifying the merging of old and the new.'

But the Met's new electric com-

partment stock trains, despite their superior comfort to the Bakerloo Tube and the LMS electric service from Watford Junction and High Street (there was also the LMS electric Croxley branch) were not as popular as Selbie had hoped. The vast crowds never came to Watford and to this day the line has an air of a rural branch line that has somehow survived.

The Met goes to Stanmore. The most rapidly built-up areas of the Underground suburbs were the places along the Metropolitan Railway line to Stanmore. The 4-mile branch from Wembley Park, with its three intermediate stations, was planned and constructed in a remarkably short space of time. The Metropolitan had often looked northwards from its main line at Wembley Park towards Edgware and even beyond. Land had at one time to be purchased for a possible Hendon line from Neasden. But the land was sold in the post-first World War period for housing. The main barrier was raising enough finance. The Government's Development (Loans and Guarantee) Act of November 1929 was a scheme to improve trade and reduce unemployment. The Metropolitan very quickly applied for a grant and its directors decided on a branch to Stanmore. The Stanmore Railway Act was passed on 4 June 1930. Despite heavy works involving diversion of the Wealdstone Brook and some deep cuttings in the slippery Middlesex clay, coupled with very wet weather, the line was completed and opened on 10 December 1932. The ceremony was performed by the Minister of Transport, P. J. Pybus. There was a special train for the VIPs and press, consisting of electric compartment stock, also the saloon carriage known as the 'Rothschild Saloon'.

Outside peak hours, each train consisted of a single electric car with cabs at each end and there were a total of 144 trains a day. Kingsbury, Canons Park and Stanmore stations were designed by C. W. Clark in his suburban villa style used on the earlier

Watford branch.

The *Harrow Observer* had a special article on the new line and mentioned that a large firm of builders were already preparing to build a huge estate on the former Stag Lane Aerodrome site, north of Kingsbury. A Golders Green estate agent announced a competition for a name to be used for a station to serve the estate and eventually the winning title was 'Queensbury'. The Queensbury Estate was to provide homes for 50,000 people and would be carefully planned, but there would be some light industry. Houses were priced between £600 and £800. The third station – Queensbury – was opened on 16 December 1934. But traffic was slow to develop. This was possibly because the Met charged main-line fares and people found it cheaper to go to Edgware by bus and take the Hampstead (Northern Line) Tube.

Queensbury became the most rapidly developed estate in the north-west. The landscape was more or less devoid of natural features. Even the few elms were cut down along Honeypot Lane (the Honey was probably a reference to the stickiness of the Middlesex mud.)

Stag Lane Aerodrome had been founded by William Warren in 1917 for war training. After the war, Amy Johnson learned to fly here for £4 an hour. The De Havilland Aircraft Company also had a plant here and built the famous Tiger Moth. But eventually, De Havillands moved their flying operations and part of the factory to Hatfield. By 1934 the land was for sale and the great estate was begun.

The principal developers were Hilbery Chaplin & Co and the Sharon Development Co, with John Laing & Co building the houses. Even as early as December 1932, the plans were being drawn up for the estate. One of the early Laing developments in the area was at Canons Park, Whitchurch Lane, where houses were advertised as being in 'beautifully wooded grounds within a few minutes of the new Canons Park Met Railway Station'.

Queensbury attracted many lower-income families who,

before that time, had not been able to afford a home of their own. They came to Queensbury because, like so many others, they wanted something more than to pay high rents all their working lives and have nothing to show for it at the end.

At Queensbury people had a small home with modern conveniences like an Ideal hot water boiler in the kitchen, a small garden and even a space for a garage. Parades of shops, with some eighty or so units to let, appeared quickly near the station and if people didn't fancy the daily ride to London, there were local firms setting up along the Honeypot Lane industrial estate.

At Kingsbury, the Met station and its flanking shops were soon all but lost in a huge length of shopping parades. There were even two cinemas by the end of the 1930s and the only open space left was Roe Green Park and the land towards Barn Hill. 'Kingsbury . . . the Queen of north-west London suburbs,' announced one developer. 'There are no steep hills, yet the estate is sufficiently high to give splendid views over the countryside.' Strangely enough, that stretch of open land has survived on both sides of Fryent Way. In 1932 Henry J. Clarke of Old Church Lane, Kingsbury, advertised his 'Ideal homes estate . . . the new addition to Metro-land . . . artistically designed houses within a few minutes of the two new Metro stations.' There was also the Audley Estate, where 'Happiness homes of quality and distinction' were available on special terms for civil servants and school teachers. F. G. Parsons & Sons assured purchasers that 'time alone will tell . . . we guarantee our houses'.

The Bakerloo takes over. The LPTB New Works plan included the project to relieve the twin tracks of the Metropolitan Line between Baker Street and Finchley Road by extending the Bakerloo Line beneath and running the tube trains on to Wembley Park over the Met's old slow local tracks, then taking over the Metropolitan service to Stanmore. The Met

stations at St John's Wood, Marlborough Road and Swiss Cottage were to be closed and replaced by two Tube stations – Marlborough Road was not replaced.

Work on this major engineering task began in April 1936, the main contractors being Charles Brand & Son Ltd. There were complex engineering problems to be overcome at Baker Street and particularly at Finchley Road. Here the parades of shops by the station had to be specially supported whilst the tunnels were rebuilt to allow the Bakerloo Tube trains to come to the surface at the approach to Finchley Road Met station. The first red trains ran to Stanmore on 20 November 1939, with seven trains an hour in peak periods. The single fare from Stanmore to Piccadilly Circus was 10d (about 4p). The old Met goods yard was closed at Stanmore and replaced by sidings for the Bakerloo trains.

The Bakerloo to Watford. Mention has already been made about the extension of the Bakerloo to Watford Junction. The LMS electric trains began at last in 1922. Development along the line from Wembley was slow at first. Industry appeared at North Wembley during the first World War and British Oxygen opened in 1918, with the well-known factory of Wrigleys Chewing Gum in 1926.

Wembley was already a rather large suburb by the time of the British Empire Exhibition of 1924–5 and Wembley Hill Estates had begun before 1914. Wembley Hill Garden Suburb was advertised in 1933 with 'houses of superior appearance and built of carefully selected materials by Messrs Callow & Wright. Only five minutes from Wembley Bakerloo Tube'. The main shopping centre was well established by the late 1920s and trams had run through to Sudbury from 1910. They were replaced by trolleybuses from 1936.

At North Wembley not all was industry. In fact, parts of the area, particularly towards the slopes of Sudbury Hill and Harrow and to South Kenton industry. In fact, parts of the (where a station was opened on the Bakerloo/LMS in 1933), there were some high-class neo-Tudor housing estates. The St Augustine Estate promised that: 'After the toil and stuffiness of the City, you will appreciate the bracing air of this beautiful, healthy suburb. Perfect sanitation.' Comben & Wakeling had already built some 1,500 houses by 1937.

Similar houses by F. & C. Costain 'Distinctive Tudor residences of quality' were also popular in this area. 'When buying a house one cannot make the decision too carefully,' they stated in their brochure. The glossy pages had artists' impressions of their detached and semi-detached houses, with names such as 'The Waverley', 'The Dorchester', 'The Mayfair', from £780.

At Kenton, Costains were also active. Another developer was H.R. & P. (London) Ltd, who built on the flat fields between Kenton and Belmont. The land had at one time been owned by Bartholomew's Hospital, London. From about 1928 H.R. & P. had an estate office near Kenton Station, and to clients who were doubtful about the wisdom of living over 1½ miles from a railway station, they emphasised that their houses were of good construction and tasteful design. The semi-detached types ranged from £825 and had shared drives for future garages. The estate spread north to Belmont, where Kenton Lane ran to the outskirts of Wealdstone. The LMS branch line to Stanmore from Wealdstone was crossed here and a halt opened in 1932. Belmont grew rapidly and soon had the inevitable shopping 'Circle' and even a cinema, the Essoldo. Wealdstone was built up in the late 19th century, but the slopes of the Weald remained the property of New College, Oxford, until the beginning of the 1930s. Then the College sold and John Searcy & Co began to develop the New College Estate, with the roads named after historical personalities connected with New College.

Standard Estates built on the northern part of Kenton Lane in 1933 and the builder of the houses, a man named Jefferies, would go round on a Sunday, when people came to visit the site, and offer to lend them the £5 deposit money! 'Houses on gently moulded hills, surrounded by verdant lanes and age-old trees, giving quiet, pastoral beauty. This is the ideal setting for one's home.' Even today some of this sylvan beauty remains.

Hatch End remained fairly open until the late 1930s and is still surrounded by Green Belt land. 'Hatch End,' remarked a guide book of the late 1920s, 'is one of those very beautiful districts with quite distinctive claims as a delightful and very desirable residential area. The surrounding countryside is both undulating and well wooded.'

Beyond Hatch End, the Hertfordshire border is crossed. Carpenders Park station opened as a halt in April 1914 to serve Oxhey Golf Course. The LCC developed a vast estate here after the second World War and the station was rebuilt in 1954. But Watford has always had a distinct identity and, with the exception of Cassiobury Park and the area near the Metropolitan station, could never properly be called an Underground suburb.

Approaching Wembley. Busy scene looking towards Neasden from the road bridge at Wembley Park station c1924. The twin chimneys of the Met power station are in the distance – a landmark for many years. The special Wembley Exhibition platform is on the left, whilst two Extension Line trains, composed of 'Dreadnought' steam stock with electric locomotives, are passing. A saloon stock train for Uxbridge is on the right.

Wembley Park. Barn Hill: Artist's impression of the Barn Hill area about 1930. In the middle can be seen the Wealdstone brook – which the artist has given river-like breadth! Later the Stanmore branch line was routed through here to Kingsbury. On the left is the original Preston Road halt (opened 21 May 1908) then sited on the Wembley side of the road bridge. The new station, with flanking shops, was completed in 1931–2.

[Grange Museum]

Kingsbury. Old Blackbird Cross – an old farm and cottages near the ancient church of St Andrew. In 1933, an impressive Victorian church was built beside it – having been removed stone by stone from Wells Street, Marylebone.

Despite the British Empire Exhibition of 1924–5 only a mile down the road, Kingsbury village remained very rural and C. W. B. Simmonds of Cricklewood advertised bungalows and villa residences 'amid charmingly rural scenery, yet less than six miles from Marble Arch, from £750 to £3,000'. There was also Kingsbury Garden Village of the Metropolitan Railway Country Estates 'laid out on the very best garden city lines' on 40 acres 'built by well established local builders'.   [Grange Museum]

To Wembley for the Cup. There will be room for all at the new stadium according to this Metropolitan poster of 1923. But so many people turned up that the pitch was invaded and it was only a policeman on a white horse, who gradually persuaded the crowds to move off the pitch, that saved the day from disaster.

The locomotive is one of the 20 constructed for the Metropolitan in 1922 for the Extension Line services. Later, No. 17 was named 'Florence Nightingale'.

Stanmore. Elms, oaks, and endless meadows greeted the builders of the line to Stanmore in 1931. A light railway track has been laid to convey materials to the various working sites.

Stanmore extension, 1932. Unidentified 0-4-0 steam locomotive with spoil wagons near the site of Queensbury. The contractors, Walter Scott & Middleton, had great difficulty in handling the sticky Middlesex clay that lay beneath the grassy countryside.

Stanmore extension. This pretty footpath across the fields to Stanmore marked almost the exact route of the new branch. This scene was taken just before the excavator got busy.

Map of the Stanmore Branch. 'The new line will pass through countryside that is essentially pastoral in character and will provide roomy, healthy and happy conditions for a considerable population, while the pleasant lanes, meadow-tracks and by-ways that abound in the district will also soon become deservedly popular with the pleasure seeker,' stated a Metropolitan country outings booklet. In the top right-hand corner, the map shows New Edgware but not the rival Hampstead Tube line. Nor is the LMS/Bakerloo Line near Northwick Park depicted.

77

Canons Park. Everybody has stopped to watch one of the giant girders, supplied by The Furness Shipbuilding Co, about to be erected at Whitchurch Lane in 1932. Soon Canons Park station buildings will appear by the bridge and there were plans for houses by Laing. Mindful of the fact that the Metropolitan charged 'main-line' fares, early Laing estate brochures stated that it was only a 1d (½p) bus ride to the Tube terminus at Edgware.

Henry J. Clare's estate was 'situated in the heart of the countryside within 10 miles of Marble Arch'. Tennis courts were to be provided including some with floodlighting. Even the rigours of the Middlesex winters could be mitigated with 'slow combustion stoves fitted in every kitchen'.

Stanmore extension. The Wealdstone Brook had to be diverted in order to avoid the railway having to cross it five times.

All stations to Stanmore. The LPTB Works Programme of 1935–6 made provision for building a branch for the Bakerloo trains from Baker Street to Finchley Road under the congested Met tracks. The Bakerloo trains then took over the Met's slow services to Wembley Park and the Stanmore branch from 1939. This picture shows a 1938 stock train with Standard type 1920s trailer approaching Kingsbury. [C. R. L. Coles]

Kingsbury. The Met's own architect, C. W. Clark, was famed for his rustic and suburban villa style of stations. But his bare platforms and their ugly lamps were in contrast to the style of the Piccadilly Line extensions on the Underground.

The stations and ancillary work on the Stanmore Line were by the Pitcher Construction Co, also Hipperston & Son Ltd.

'From the outset, the intention is to develop the area residentially, and there will be shops, schools, and churches . . . the amenities so necessary to the growth of a large community,' said the Metropolitan publicity.

Other literature enthused: 'Palaces built of rustic bricks in avenues of trees that will grow more beautiful as the years pass.' By 1939 acre upon acre of 'palaces' had filled all the land, except that on the western slopes of Barn Hill, where open spaces are preserved along Fryent Way until the present day.

Stanmore: Official opening train on the Metropolitan's new branch to Stanmore, 9th December 1932. The third vehicle is the Met's Director's Saloon, with a Pullman car behind.

Wembley

Most builders termed their developments 'Garden Suburbs' or 'Garden City' if they had taken some sort of effort to provide a parade of shops on their new estates. This typical advertisement for Callow & Wright shows what was on offer at Wembley Hill, near to the Bakerloo Line.

Harrow-on-the-Hill. The old two-platform station of 1880 was enlarged in 1908. Total reconstruction began in 1938 and this view shows the LNER Aylesbury platform partly rebuilt. But the final completion of the Harrow project, with six tracks, did not take place until 1948.

CINEMA AND PARADE, NORTH HARROW.

NORTH HARROW

Baker Street - - - 10¾ *Miles.*

NORTH HARROW has grown up round the Metropolitan Station—now an up-to-date building of the latest type. The changes effected here in the last five years have been as remarkable as any in the outer London area, the population having more than doubled.

The old high road from Harrow to Pinner is unrecognisable at this point save for the sharp rectangular turn at the now forgotten Hooking Bridge Green. It has become a broad and comely High Street.

On both sides of the line attractive avenues are being laid out with pleasant vistas and gardening would seem to be a universal hobby. On the south side a fine new 80 ft. wide arterial road will ultimately be carried through to Ealing.

North Harrow may congratulate itself on being born late, when it compares its amenities with those of any London suburb which was developed even a dozen years ago.

A TYPICAL ROAD, NORTH HARROW.

North Harrow. A page from *Metro-land* showing the amenities of the new North Harrow at the start of the 1930s. The Embassy Cinema opened in September 1929, the ceremony being performed by actress Betty Balfour. Vast crowds queued to get into the cinema, which was floodlit. The old hamlet of Hooking Green that once stood here was forgotten, but the stream culverted beneath the cinema had its revenge by bursting through into the stalls on several occasions during storms in later years!

Northwick Park. Advertisement, in 1927, for the estate built on land owned by the Churchill Family, whose seat was at Northwick Park near Blockley in the Cotswolds. The Met Country Estates announced: 'Why pay high rents and live in crowded flats when well-planned houses can be purchased on advantageous terms.

THE NORTHWICK ESTATE
NORTHWICK PARK & KENTON

LONDON'S NEW SUBURB

9 miles from the Marble Arch.
14 minutes from Baker Street.
Served by three Electric Railways.
Over 100 Trains each way every day.

A UNIQUE SPECIMEN OF TOWN PLANNING

The Largest and best laid out Estate near London.

Delightful & Artistic Freehold Houses for Sale

Each a distinctive Ideal Home in every sense of the word.
Splendidly built, only the best material being used.
Perfect rural surroundings, Lovely views, Extraordinarily healthy.
Well constructed Roads. Main Drainage. Electric Light and Gas, and Colne Valley Water.

WOODCOCK HILL LANE.

Harrow. Station Road c1938, with the Coliseum Theatre, which opened as a cinema on 11 October 1920. The ceremony was performed by a certain Oswald Moseley MP. Later the building, with its American soda fountain was taken over by Alfred Denville who presented a popular mixture of ballet, opera and and concerts through the war years. The building was demolished in the late 1950s.

In the distance is an ST-type bus on the 140 route to Hayes.

Alternative travel: Harrow. By the late 1930s, the Green Line coach network duplicated many Underground suburban lines. Here a T-type coach on the Amersham-Harrow-Victoria-Wrotham service approaches the stop near Harrow Met station in about 1949. The villas in the background have now been replaced by faceless office blocks.

[C. R. L. Coles]

Ruislip Manor. Reconstructing the Metropolitan bridge at Victoria Road, 1936–7. A Baker Street-bound train of 'T' stock is slowing down for the station, whilst a Piccadilly Line train for Uxbridge is just pulling out.

[L. Marsden]

Ruislip. A rustic scene in Sharps Lane in the 1920s.

Ruislip Manor Estate. Looking up Victoria Road towards the station c1933. George Ball's Manor Homes Estate office is the large structure on the right. Outside stands one of the motor cars waiting to take prospective buyers to the more distant parts of the estate. Left is a large hut that looks as if it was the site drawing-office.

Visitors to the estate were urged 'to make of one of our salesmen all their enquiries which are so essential to later satisfaction . . . we will reserve a plot (or house, if available) for a period of 7 to 14 days'.

Ruislip. Not long after the Metropolitan station opened in 1904, the first developments began. But the houses were of villa-type, and blended well in the rural lanes near the village, as this scene in Sharps Lane shows.

Ruislip. Looking towards the station from Wood Lane bridge in 1936, with 4-car train made up of 'T' stock motor car and saloon type trailers. [L. Marsden]

Ruislip Manor. Modern construction methods were a feature of the Manor Homes Estate: concrete roads laid down ahead of the houses and even a light railway system to carry the materials from the Met sidings all the way to distant parts of the estate. In the background are the hedges and trees of the old fields that are very shortly to be buried forever beneath the hygienic concrete and tarmac. But the buyers of Manor Homes thought little of that, despite the brochures that urged: 'Travelling for only half-an-hour or so from London, you will find an estate still retaining the unmarred beauties – and the unspoiled healthy atmosphere of Nature in her most beautiful aspects.'

Ruislip Manor. Houses like these on the left were of slightly varied design. An end-terraced home with three bedrooms, fitted with the high tech of electric wall fires in the bedrooms, and a parlour-kitchenette, cost from £470.

The piles of window and door frames were manufactured in the Company's own joinery works at Wealdstone. At one time the Ruislip Manor contract was employing nearly 1,000 men.

Manor Homes advertisement 1934. Not everybody liked this kind of advertisement nor the houses that the Nash group of companies built. At Rayners Lane, E. S. Reid's Harrow Garden Village Estate announced in *Metro-land*: 'Profit is not the first consideration . . . our houses are not blots on the landscape . . . great care has been taken to keep away from the monotony of mass-produced houses.'

Fireworks! On 30 September 1933 the London *Evening News* advertised: 'Free tonight! Bring your friends to see the great firework and searchlight display at Ruislip Manor.' There was a collection in aid of local hospitals. One cannot help feeling that the finale, with its display of a London lit up with a Zeppelin, was foreshadowing a London lit up by more sinister aircraft only seven years later.

Ruislip Manor. Passengers had to be careful as they left the halt during the 1936–7 reconstruction works. The halt (which first opened on 5 August 1912) was rebuilt in June 1938, although the platform reconstruction was never completed.

[L. Marsden]

Ickenham. Improvements in Swakeleys Road 1936. Preparations are under way for widening the road and easing the sharp bend at the junction with The Avenue. The reconstruction of roads was a major task for local authorities as the Underground suburbs grew up.

Ickenham. The history of local bus services in the outer suburbs is often obscure. The first bus to run from Uxbridge to Ickenham and Ruislip, then to Pinner, was in 1929. It was operated by the Loumax Company via Long Lane. Later this service was London General Route 505.

The Royal Highlander Co. of South Harrow ran several routes, and their service 81 from Uxbridge to Pinner, via Swakeleys Road, began in the spring of 1931. In LPTB days, in January 1936, this 17-seater Dennis Dart had to negotiate floods by the River Pinn. The 223 bus route ran this way to Ruislip Manor in 1937.

Ruislip station, showing the typical lattice-style footbridge found at most Metropolitan stations. Note the semaphore signal in dropped position to allow a train into the station, bound for Uxbridge.

South Harefield. This was the site of a proposed halt on the GWR/LNER line to High Wycombe. The station was about mid-way between West Ruislip and Denham. The estate agent's picture shows plot numbers reserved for shops. The halt opened between 24 September 1928 and September 1931, but attracted little traffic. The proposed Central Line extension to Denham would have had a station here. Today the bridge and road have changed little and the countryside still sweeps down to the Colne valley.

Ickenham. Developments in Swakeleys Road at the Harefield Place Estate in 1939: 'The healthiest, and best spot in the district.' The arrow to the left of the board directs the visitor to their estate office in Highfield Drive. The grounds of Harefield Place were developed with individually designed houses on large plots for 'those seeking a residential estate near enough to London to be handy, yet far enough as to be truly rural . . . an estate where modern efficiency happily mingles with the old'.

Ickenham. Swakeleys Road towards the Pinn bridge in May 1930. Houses have been built on the right-hand side, reached by footbridges over the open ditch. Within seven years all was built up, with a dual carriageway and houses on both sides.

Ickenham station. This 1933 picture shows a typical Metropolitan halt with its street-level booking hut (still in use at Hillingdon). There were once similar arrangements at Rayners Lane and Eastcote. A contrast to the Underground extensions to Edgware and Cockfosters.

Ickenham. It is almost inconceivable that cottages like this were still being lived in at a time when the Metropolitan was being built to Uxbridge. One of the small boys in this picture of members of the Winch family was reported missing in the first World War. Then, much to the joy of everybody in the village, Albert returned! The cottages were replaced by the Village War Memorial Hall.   [Miss F. Winch]

Building the Central Line. Ruislip Gardens and the new bridge under construction 1940. Despite the blackout, orders were given by the GWR (who were responsible for constructing this branch of the Central Line) to turn on the floodlights and finish the job overnight! Despite nearby RAF Northolt, nobody called 'put that light out' and the job was finished. But shortage of materials and labour eventually brought work to an end until after the war.

Uxbridge. The original Belmont Road terminus was a contrast to the classical villa style of Edgware or Morden! But Uxbridge was never really an Underground suburb in Metropolitan days. The arrival of the new electric line in 1904 was regarded as a way of boosting local trade and helping to support a plan for a South Bucks and Middlesex cattle market.

Hillingdon. Year after year there were rumours and plans for extending the Central Line, and even the Piccadilly, from Ealing to Hayes and on to Uxbridge. But the trams had to take all the traffic. This 'Feltham' type car is seen near Hillingdon Heath, bound for Uxbridge, about 1933. The trams were replaced by trolleybuses in 1936.

Ickenham. Swakeleys Road shortly before work began on the dual carriageway which was completed in 1937.

Kenton. Costain's yard, South Kenton 1933, with LMS lines on right. The private sidings for delivery of building supplies was a feature of many builders' yards at this period.

Costain built much of South Kenton. The types of houses advertised had impressive names such as 'The Dorchester', 'The Waverley', 'The Mayfair'. Prices were high – up to £3500. By January 1939, building costs were rising due to War preparations and in Costain's last brochure there was an overprint warning 'General price increase £25.' The yard lasted until the early 1960s.

[Grange Museum]

Wembley. The old and the new: ancient cottages next to modern semi-detached houses in East Lane c1934. [Grange Museum]

North Harrow. By 1938 North Harrow was a complete suburb and had a vast array of shops. This photograph shows an STD-type bus at the stop near the Embassy Cinema just after the second World War. In the distance you can see an impressive building with a clock tower, at the beginning of one of the long shopping parades that stretched towards Headstone Lane. [C. R. L. Coles]

Wembley. Watford-bound Bakerloo train about 1920, composed of the new 'Watford Joint Stock', built by the Metropolitan Carriage and Wagon Co Ltd. The cars were then the longest on the Underground, being 50ft 10in. They had sliding doors, comfortable pairs of seats and even luggage racks.   [Charles R. Gordon-Stuart]

Wealdstone. One of the Oerlikon electric trains of the LNWR, introduced in July 1922, leaving Wealdstone on 28 May 1957. Trains of this type (also a compartment variety) were used on the LMS suburban electric services until the early 1960s. There were branches in the Watford area to Rickmansworth and to Croxley – the latter is still open. [C. R. L. Coles]

Neasden. The *Sunday Referee* placard announces with confidence in the future: 'Good News from Germany.' This is 1933 and the driver of the car is no doubt more concerned with the imminent arrival of Aunt Maud for her Sunday lunch than what Herr Hitler is going to do. The station buildings date from 1880 when the name was 'Kingsbury & Neasden'. As Neasden grew and the streeets of Edwardian houses crept up the slopes of Dudding Hill and Dollis Hill, the names were reversed. On 1 January 1932, the name 'Kingsbury' was dropped with the impending opening of the Stanmore branch.

Neasden grew rapidly in the late 1920s; vast estates of terraced houses covered the high meadows above the new North Circular Road and Kingsbury Reservoir ('the Welsh Harp'). The famous old inn 'The Spotted Dog' was 'neo-Tudorised' and old Neasden House, a Regency mansion described in 1850 as being situated 'in a quiet and elevated position on the slopes of Dolleys (*sic*) Hill' gave way to parades of garish shops. The Grange, an old farmhouse, survived behind its brick boundary walls to become the delightful Grange Museum of local history.

These Metropolitan station buildings were highly praised when first erected. A columnist wrote in *Harper's Magazine* of the extension of the Underground to Harrow: ' "By Underground to Harrow" is the legend that confronts the lingering Londoner at many of the local railway stations in the West End. It is a misnomer, referring to the extension of the Underground system of railway to Harrow, but from Baker Street, with the exception of two insignificant tunnels, the track runs through open country . . . Every railway station or depot at which the train stops to Harrow is a red-brick picture – a modest adaptation of "Old Kensington" to the most practical purpose. Platforms, waiting rooms, the buildings generally are constructed with an eye to beauty as well as usefulness.'

Harrow. Try Harrow: a London Transport advertisement of summer, 1933. The press advertisements of the newly-formed organisation were quite remarkable for the high quality of illustrations. Here an athletic Lowry-type female pushes a hand-mower rapidly up a slope while a gardener, serf-like, strains forward with a heavy load of soil, shaping the new suburb. The Underground was prepared to issue lists of local estate agents, in its drive for new traffic.

Carpenders Park. Bakerloo Line train of 1938 stock with a 'Standard' trailer departing on 7 June 1960. It is passing an LMR electric set.

[C. R. L. Coles]

Willesden Junction. 5-car Bakerloo train during the first World War. It is made up of two 1915-type motor cars borrowed from the Central London Line, with gate-ended trailer cars from the Piccadilly Line. Because of the labour shortage, the gates of each car are operated by women.

Kenton. HRP estate advertisement. The land was sold by St
Bartholomew's Hospital for building in about 1929 and over the next five
years the vast estate of neat semi-detached houses spread right across
from Kenton Lane to the edge of Wealdstone and north
towards Belmont.

Kenton, with its parades of shops, its houses with their gardens full of
roses, and the old Wealdstone brook safely culverted, was the complete
suburb. The only countryside was glimpsed away north on the slopes of
Harrow Weald.

Kenton. The station bridge in 1933. The Estate Developer's boards
advertise the HRP Estate off Christchurch Avenue, for which Edwards
were the estate agents. They had an office in one of the wooden huts
seen here. Adjacent were coal offices – one merchant had a giant lump of
coal set in his forecourt and samples of the types of coals displayed in
model railway wagons in the window.

J. Warner, the florist, was next to the station for many years and
home-coming husbands at Saturday lunchtime would buy bunches of
flowers here. One of the authors can remember the smell of flowers
mingling with the Jeyes fluid used in the station, combined with the
steam of the passing LMS trains.

Over the bridge, beyond the Underground sign, was the bus stop
outside the Rest Hotel. How comforting it used to be when, peering
through the drizzle of a December teatime, the lights and peaked roof of
an ST-type bus appeared, to take a small boy home to tea by an open
fire, with the 'Ovaltinees' on the wireless! But one day he recalls reading
the funny word 'Warsaw' and asking why it was in such big letters on the
newsboy's bill-board outside the station.

Note the early compressor at work with a road team forming a new
island (since gone). Even in the 1930s, many roads were still being
opened by teams using cold chisels held with huge steel tongs, with a pair
of workmen striking the head of the tool in succession with a heavy
sledge hammer.

Watford Junction. It must be a Sunday, because even for the 1930s there is little road traffic about! Until recently the station had remained much as it is here. The temperance cafe on the right survived until the late 1970s. Both LMS electric and Underground signs can be seen.

Ruislip. State of war: the ARP post and the fire station are all equipped for the bombers, and the days of buying houses on the Park Avenue and Broadwood Avenue Estates advertised on the boards have come to an end.

A. V. Low's last message as the sirens sounded was: 'You can buy one of the detached houses at the end of the road, but no money can buy the beautiful woods,' a belated acknowledgement of the damage done by thoughtless building during the 1930s.   [L. Marsden]

RIDGEWAY ESTATE
NORTH HARROW

Built by CUTLERS
BUILDERS FOR 20 YEARS IN THIS DISTRICT

Walk into a Cutler house on the Ridgeway Estate at North Harrow. Examine it carefully—the design, construction, soundness of it all. HERE *IS* VALUE! It almost "sells itself"! Your Surveyor will approve it. Brick built, semi-detached, 3 bedrooms, room for garage. Estate next station. 17 mins. from Baker Street, 30 mins. City.

From £795. Larger type £895 (as illustrated). Detached from £950. 90% of mortgage can be arranged. Convenient weekly repayments. No road charges or law costs. Special terms to Civil Servants, Bank Officials, Railway and Insurance Officials, L.C.C. Staff Association.

Write NOW for illustrated booklet and FREE TRAVELLING VOUCHER from Baker Street.

Builders,

12, STATION ROAD, NORTH HARROW
Telephone : HARROW 0139

SAY YOU SAW IT IN "METRO-LAND."

North Harrow. Cutlers built some 7,000 houses in the North Harrow district in a period of about 25 years, starting before 1914. Living at North Harrow was given an extra air of security by one of Cutler's advertisements: 'Many of our houses have been purchased by surveyors, bankers and architects.' No doubt they were attracted by the superb stained-glass windows in every hall and landing. There was a choice of designs: sailing ships; lighthouses and sea gulls; windmills; and the inevitable sunrise. Surely, these rows of semi-detached houses in their narrow road overhung by flowering trees, the gardens full of rustic trellis and roses, capture the very essence of Metro-land.

4

INTO THE SUNSET: THE WESTERN AND SOUTHERN SUBURBS

The Piccadilly Line to Uxbridge.
With the completion of the Underground railway improvements between Hammersmith and Acton Town, there were four tracks available. The outer lines were to be used by the District stopping services, the two inner pair for non-stop Piccadilly trains between these two places. The Piccadilly trains commenced running to South Harrow on 4 July 1933; the running time between Finsbury Park and South Harrow was 34 minutes. On 23 October 1933, the service was extended over the viaduct to Rayners Lane and on to Uxbridge, providing a joint service with the Metropolitan between the latter two places.

The Tube trains looked strangely diminutive standing beside the 'main-line' sized Metropolitan saloon or compartment stock. But the passengers soon began to use the Tube service and its alternative route to the heart of the West End.

The old Park Royal station was replaced by a station sited on the Western Avenue at the junction near Hanger Hill from 5 July 1931. The station buildings by Day, Welch & Lander were completed in permanent form in March 1936. The tall tower, with its London Transport symbol, became a conspicuous landmark for local people and the employees of the new factories then being built in that area.

Alperton was rebuilt in 1931, and a bus garage erected next door. But it was the next station along the line that was to become famous as the summit of Underground architecture of the period. Sudbury Town by Charles Holden was completed in July 1931. Its lofty booking hall, with tall windows, its bronze lamp fittings and its illuminated station name (since removed) were much admired. There was an ample turning space for buses outside and even provision for a cafe.

Sudbury Hill and South Harrow were also rebuilt. At South Harrow the new station was sited by the shopping centre in Northolt Road, the buildings being below the Roxeth viaduct. Once again there was a bus turning space. The inhabitants of the long rows of new terraced houses at Northolt Park, Northolt, and along the seemingly interminable Whitton Avenue from Sudbury, could hop on a bus and be taken straight to the Tube stations along the line rather than use the old-fashioned and sooty steam trains of the LNER Marylebone Line (Sudbury Hill [Harrow] station and Sudbury [Harrow Road] were very close to the Piccadilly Line), or from Northolt on the GWR.

The quiet and flat countryside near South Harrow with Harrow Hill rising majestically to the north, attracted day trippers from early District Railway days. Northolt Road was a pleasant country by-way and thousands of children and adults visited The Paddocks, not far from the present day Alexandra Avenue and Northolt Park station. At The Paddocks were thirty acres of grounds full of attractions such as roundabouts, donkey rides, see-saws, picnic areas and a miniature railway. When the tea gardens finally closed, part of the land was incorporated into the new Alexandra Park.

As late as 1931 the area remained fairly rural and purchasers of new houses were told: 'The visitor with a love for picturesque houses will be pleased with the charming dairy farmhouse not far from the station on the Northolt Road; cream-washed and many-gabled, gay with borders of well-formed flowers and climbing roses.'

Developments along the 'Long Mile', which was renamed Eastcote Lane, began in the early 1920s. Eventually, the vast T. F. Nash Rayners Lane Estate was to link up at a number of places. Other builders were also hard at work in the late 1930s, covering every square foot of meadow land, felling every tree they could get their saws across, until they finally achieved complete ruin of the landscape from the LNER Marylebone Line at Field End Road to the shops at South Harrow.

Westward to Hounslow. The extension of the Piccadilly Line over the District tracks to Hounslow was through an area that had been comparatively undisturbed by the growing restlessness of the immediate post-war period of the 1920s. The District branch had run through flat fields and market gardens for much of its route to Hounslow. But plans were being put in hand for a modern trunk road that would by-pass the traffic bottlenecks of Brentford and Hounslow and take the growing motor traffic directly out towards Staines and north Surrey. This arterial highway, called the Great West Road, had been an idea as far back as the early 1900s – one of its instigators was Lord Montagu, the motoring pioneer. The Great West Road encouraged ribbon development of generally high-class housing.

The road was revolutionary for England at that time, with provision for cycle tracks – the forerunner of the separated traffic systems of modern towns. Surrounded by fast new District and Piccadilly trains – and the new road – the areas of Syon and Osterley quickly filled up.

In 1935 Hounslow seemed to be hardly aware of the new role that the age of the common man had cast upon it – the service area of a vast dormitory linked to London. The old High Street was still lined by comfortable old inns and quaint shops, although some old drapers' businesses were then modernising to offer complete home-fitting departments. They were Edmonds (Bon Marché) and Murfitts. Between them was a bustle of tiny grocers' and hardware shops, with the stores of old-established grocery chains such as David Greig, Maypole (where butter could be knocked up with wooden bats and impressed with a pattern selected by the customer), and Star International – full of flavours and aromas of the East.

Outside, the electric trams hurried by to take home those people who lived in the older districts of Isleworth and Busch Corner. The trams were soon replaced by smart new trolleybuses, which swept by to their new terminus further along the Staines

Road. Here a special turning circle had been constructed for them at the 'Wellington', public house.

The tremendous impact of housing development west of Hounslow came with the extension of the Piccadilly Line service. Two additional tracks were constructed between Acton Town and Northfields and the work completed on 18 December 1932. The Piccadilly trains reached Northfields on 9 January 1933 and a huge new depot was constructed here. The final extension was opened to Hounslow West on 13 March 1933.

Between 1933 and the outbreak of the second World War, all the land between the Hounslow West terminus and Harlington (with the exception of some pockets of land) was built over. The stations along the Hounslow Line were improved at this time, with a keen appreciation of the linking role between car, bus and train that was to develop so rapidly during the 1950s and after.

The old District Railway station known as Osterley & Spring Grove was closed in 1934 and a modern Underground station called Osterley was erected at the intersection of the new Great West Road, half-a-mile westwards. Both the new stations at Osterley (with its illuminated tower) and Hounslow West (with its wide circulating area) looked their best at night, the illuminated fascias and dome of Hounslow West station being visible for a great distance. It seemed to anticipate, with its use of a roundel of defused light, the modern impression of a flying saucer.

Although passengers at Hounslow East had a miserable wait on their draughty and exposed platform until the new waiting room and canopy were put up in 1965, by the summer of 1933 the Hounslow services offered fast trains both by District and Piccadilly Line trains. They linked the new commuters living west of Hounslow to the centre of London within 40 minutes or so. By then the whole of the market gardens and orchards were disappearing, at an ever-accelerating rate, under bricks and mortar.

It was still possible, even after 1934, to step outside Hounslow West station and very soon walk in semi-countryside. By the 1930s most of the land between Hounslow Town and the Barracks had been built over, but a broad band of pasture stretched unbroken towards the junction with the new Great West Road, with the exception of a Victorian cottage, which suffered a direct hit by one of the first V2 rockets in the war.

The land that bordered the northern side of the Bath Road was under market garden cultivation. This area was about to be built over as the second World War began (the builders' huts were then used as a greengrocers, selling produce from the land immediately behind it). About this time, the 'Travellers Friend' public house at the end of the Great West Road became an important stopping place for motor drivers and for buses running towards Slough and Windsor, along the Bath Road.

Beyond, the Bath Road ran westwards towards the village of Cranford as a wide and tree-lined tarmac highway used by the occasional motor car. By a curious turn of fate, the vast fields on the north side of the Bath Road at this point, which were known as 'Hundred Acres', remain in part to this day as open land. They give some glimpse of what life was like in the area fifty years ago. At the 'Berkeley Arms' a dusty lane led northward towards the sleepy hamlet of Cranford. In 1933 this was a thoroughfare lined with enormous trees of great age.

From the Georgian and Regency mansions that lined this lane to Cranford emerged, rather timidly, the occasional Rolls Royce or Rover. The occupants of these houses were about to be surrounded by the noise of concrete mixers and walls of bricks and tiles. The Berkeley family, who had owned old Cranford House for generations, left their wonderful Georgian mansion to its fate about this time. Their estate, known as Cranford Park, was taken over for public use, the land being administered jointly by the Heston & Isleworth Borough Council and the Hayes &

Harlington Council. It was to prove a valuable green 'lung' for the new 'frontiers-people' of the suburbs.

Cranford stood on the Bath Road, but mail coaches did not pass through until 1784. In years gone by, however, there were hundreds of horses stabled in nearby inns. Post chaises could be seen moving along the Bath Road for over a century. Just beyond, there were broad wheatfields and large orchards providing for the London markets. The Cranford meadows had been wild heathland until the Enclosures began about 1820. Until 1850, teams of oxen drew ploughs through the Cranford Estate, and the rural picture of this part of West Middlesex was completed by sturdy Shropshire lads who had migrated from the Welsh borders by working the canal boats. They stayed in the Heston area to work as labourers. But the 20th century had arrived with a vengeance, and only the Hundred-Acre land still remains open east of Cranford to remind us of that lost Arcadia.

Beyond Cranford Bridge, the Bath Road swept on, passing the flat market gardens around Harmondsworth and Sipson – land which now supports Heathrow Airport.

As late as 1935 in this rural backwater it was a common sight to see old gentlemen riding ancient cycles, including pennyfarthings, along the lanes around Harmondsworth, almost over the area now occupied by Heathrow's International Terminal Buildings.

Local builders sound their siren calls. It was possible to rent a modern 1930s-style house within a small distance of Hounslow High Street in 1933 for 24s 0d (£1.20p) weekly. These houses had three bedrooms, separate WC and even a garage space. But most of the new working-class house buyers were interested in owning their houses for the first time – the start of what is now called a 'property owning democracy'. The rented houses were often, in fact, parts of the estate which had not been successfully sold off under mortgage, for there were already large numbers of different estates springing up. During 1934 alone, 35,000 houses had been built in the Metropolitan Water Board Area, and house building was to break all records with the improved Underground services to Hounslow.

To the north, around Heston, R. T. Warren was erecting houses which soon gained a good reputation for quality. Warren was also building further north at Hillingdon and Ickenham, Hayes and Uxbridge. His slogan was: 'Take a form of security in bricks and mortar.' His houses in the Heston area in March 1933 sold for £525 freehold in Cranford Lane. (Handy for the busy Heston Airfield where Neville Chamberlain was to land five years later, after his visit to Hitler.) In the immediate vicinity of Hounslow West station you could visit, in Easter 1935, the last few houses still for sale that had been put up by G. T. Crouch on the site of a lovely old orchard. The Crouch houses were of good standard, semi-detached at a time when more and more terraced houses (blocks of four or six) were being erected to secure a lower individual selling price. They were decorated with imitation timber and had leaded glass in bays overlooking the main road – a respectable distance away. The Crouch houses were £799 and had garage spaces. Few of the new houses actually boasted garages. House buyers were not expected to be able to afford to run a car as well as to repay their mortgages. But 'garage space' was sought by many forward-looking purchasers with an eye to the coming motor-car age.

The new Ford Popular could be seen that year in quite large numbers and cost only £115 (£6 tax). In an age when the choice lay between a baby and a baby car, there were many 'modern' couples who elected to have the car and perhaps afford a mortgage as well.

Crouch houses were soon being built elsewhere around Hounslow. By 1938 Crouch Homes on the Kneller Hall Estate at Twickenham had been reduced to £825

(bungalows £735) and in common with other speculators in the area, Mr Crouch was offering extras, including free furniture!

W. J. Harris was, arguably, the biggest builder in the Hounslow West area. He exploited the great flat acres of orchard and market garden (with the occasional gravel pit) that stretched beckoningly westward.

First, he had built around the immediate station area before spreading westwards towards the road to Cranford mentioned earlier. Here, on the south side of the Bath Road, Harris developed his extensive Cranford Manor Estate, which at one time threatened to reach south as far as the Great South Road. This was another arterial road – and was really an extension of the Great West Road. In the previous ten years, Harris had been responsible for building over 2,000 houses around Hounslow. They were of terraced design, with slate damp courses and small variations in style from block to block, mostly in regard to exterior decoration. There were assorted porches, different coloured glass in the front door panels, and an assortment of designs of wooden fencing separating the houses.

End-of-terrace houses (which shared a driveway to give 'garage space') were priced at £575 freehold in 1935, whilst others in the block went at £550 and £565.

These Harris houses were strongly built with brick partition walls between rooms, quarry-tiled kitchens (which were fitted with a free dresser and copper clothes boiler) and a back-boiler coal fire. The builder offered a choice of colours for the tiled fire-surround and houses were completely painted and decorated to choice, although buyers were warned 'to choose plain wallpapers'.

Purchasers of houses in the Cranford Manor Estate could expect to pay a mortgage repayment of about 16s 0d (80p) weekly in 1935, and a house could be secured with a deposit of only £5 down. Repayments were to be over a period of twenty-one years.

The old 'Berkeley Arms' in the Bath Road, at the start of the new

Harris Estate, exploded into French Chateau style (à la Chambord), with the parade of shops also sporting round towers and pretty blue-grey roof tiles. In the centre of the parade was a modern afterthought – a petrol station which the builder had finished with a thatched roof!

Nearer Cranford village arose the more splendid 'semis', built by Laing and priced some £200 above the Harris houses and at a lesser density per acre. At this point the Underground terminus was well over twenty minutes' walk away but developers continued to exploit the virgin land up and beyond the River Crane.

W. Grenville Collins started his Cranford Cross Estate in this area with even lower prices in 1936 – advertising homes from as little as £420 or only 10s 3d (51p) weekly.

For those housebuyers who sought to work in London, a long cycle ride or walk to Hounslow West station stared them grimly in the face as the price for buying such cheap contentment.

But soon the new estates went out even further into the once remote Middlesex countryside, covering fields and orchards, low-lying ground, and even land which was surrounded by the many gravel workings which dotted the land between Hounslow and the Thames at Staines.

The old village of Feltham was soon lost under housing, which reached out dusty fingers to Shepperton, Staines and those parts of the county which could be regarded as within reach of the Southern Railway.

Hounslow Heath, a notorious haunt of highwaymen who had preyed on coach traffic on its way from London to Bath or Southampton, remained, but by then it was a very seedy piece of open land west of Hounslow. Beyond it, in 1935, grew up Crouch's Harlington Road Estate consisting of terraced blocks. The estate was claimed to be six minutes from Feltham station, but in the summer of 1935, a prospective house buyer had only to appear outside Hounslow East or Central stations and step into one of several rather grand (and always black) saloon cars provided by the developer to transport them to those rather remote estates. Crouch offered, as an incentive, 'much lower payments' and urged buyers to 'take advantage of the drop in payments'.

'Why go on handing over 15s 0d (75p) a week or more in rent?' he argued, 'when for less than that you can have a fully equipped modern home?' It was an attractive bait to Londoners, who at that time, perhaps were paying on average 10s 6d (52½p) to 12s 6d (62½p) a week rent for two rather small rooms in the central area of Battersea, Dalston and Willesden.

Crouch's terraced houses sold for £499 (with a four-bedroomed version going for £512 in the summer of 1935). But the emphasis here was always on a weekly repayment figure of anything from 12s 8d (63½p) to 13s 0d (65p). Small wonder that, as things started to pick up a little after the 1930 Depression, those who were in work found themselves being whisked through Hounslow High Street and out to the new building, seated in the back of a fine motor car, probably the first they had ever ridden in!

This transporting of prospective house buyers was attacked by those builders near the Hounslow stations, such as the developers of the large Great West Road houses (£825 with four bedrooms and a garage). They advertised 'No car required to view these houses, which are only one or two minutes' walk from the Underground station.'

A major problem with new buyers was the lack of provision for school children. The primitive village schools were obviously quite unable to cope, and children moving into the district around Hounslow and elsewhere had to go by bus into the town schools which were soon overcrowded.

A spirit of 'New Frontier' swept the new mortgage buyers settling in. There was the usual rush of competition for custom from the milkmen (each with his horse and cart) and bakers. Neighbours, almost completely without cars or other transport, except cycles, would club together in little

collectives to purchase for joint use things such as sweeps' brushes and ladders for the maintenance of their homes.

But one builder – Clifford – claimed in 1938 to have overcome the schools problem with his grandiose-sounding estate called the 'Hounslow Garden Suburb'. This large building scheme had taken land even further from Hounslow – the great flat plain between Feltham and the Hatton Estates of W. Grenville Collins. Some concern had been shown by the local authorities about the lack of space and the density of houses, after allowing the necessary estate 'sweeps', and this point was considered when these semi-detached houses (all with garage spaces) went up for a very reasonable £465 each (weekly repayments 12s 0d (60p). But it is doubtful whether many believed the claim of the builders that a 'great new garden city is arising, having something like 2,000 houses, schools, and its own shopping centre, which when complete, will be one of the finest examples of town planning in London'. The houses, with their 1938-style steel-framed swept windows, soon lined the main Staines Road, giving it a 'dignified and attractive appearance'.

Feltham had seen earlier housing schemes, Council inspired, which had failed. Early in 1929 it had been moved in Council that £227,000 be borrowed for the erection of 500 houses in Feltham. It was said at that time that the demand for houses there was very great. But this statement was made at the start of the Great Depression, and whilst the demand may have been there, few people could do anything about it.

By the middle of 1930, fewer than 230 of these houses were occupied and there things stuck, with costs soaring, so that decisions about action were not taken and a huge deficit had to be faced. The scheme had come too early. But by 1938, the whole of the Feltham area was alive with builders' lorries and carts, successfully selling a vast range of housing to the working class.

The Bedfont Gravel Company's

land was used for bungalows by the New Ideal Homestead Group, although the company was prevented from building too close to the open pits. It had to restrict itself to a pattern of twelve homes to the acre over the whole of the building land there.

The rush for bungalows was on with a vengeance between Feltham and Staines during the second part of 1938. Over half the Spring Farm Estate sold in four months, whilst at Shepperton, C. Davis' bungalows on his Orchard Estate, complete with a gas refrigerator (a new gimmick) and terrazzo flooring, could be had for £695. The additional attraction offered by Davis was that his places were 'on the River Thames, with all the fascination of river sport at your door'. They were claimed to be two minutes' walk from the station.

It would have been strange indeed if this complete change to the face of West Middlesex which happened during the course of twenty years or so was able to take place without some sadness; perhaps by those who took up the promise of a new house away from London grime and who were unable to keep up the payments. Or perhaps by nature lovers and those lamenting the lost pastoral pleasure that Middlesex offered, and which Sir John Betjeman voiced in his poetic trip to the borders of the county 'where a few surviving hedges keep alive our lost Elysium – rural Middlesex again'.

But, oddly enough, there were some casualties in the building trade itself, as everybody wanted to get on the bandwagon and 'go for gold'. In 1933, for example, a builder working in Chestnut Grove, Isleworth, found himself charged with putting up a house that was not built upon a secure foundation as 'every house must be built upon solid rock or sub-structure'. The result for this man was bankruptcy! Some builders failed simply by over-reaching themselves in the grab for more and more land.

William Hope, who lived up to his name, was one such example. He was a simple carpenter and joiner and had presumably worked his trade without trouble during the 1920s. But in 1928 he fell in with a speculative builder in the Southall and Hayes areas, where he erected four houses, which returned an overall profit of £400. The speculator (and his know-how) then disappeared and Hope continued with the venture, erecting another 34 houses in the Hounslow area. He lost £25 on this effort, and continued to slide until he found himself in Court.

There he was able to say: "This loss did not show any lack of ability on our part. No! If I could have gone straight ahead with the job, I should have been all right. But this Clerk of Works made us alter and pull things down.'

The Judge interjected: 'You seem to imply that every builder, if he were allowed to build a house his own way, could build it for twopence, but when an architect supervises the work it can cost £1,000.' There was no reply. The judge looked at him gravely: 'Is *that* what you mean?' 'Yes,' said Hope simply.

It was a case that not only showed the need for some sort of practical building control, but also showed the lack of understanding between the builder trying to cut his costs and the architect who worked for the expensive property buyer.

The second World War saved the rest of the open land around Hounslow from further exploitation. After 1945 there was a rash of council houses that broke out around the Beavers Lane area and the old pig farm, between the 'Traveller's Friend' and the 'Jolly Waggoner' on the Bath Road, known as Rectory Farm. The completion of the Parkway Road between Hayes and Feltham and the building of London's Heathrow Airport completed the rest of the over-building. Even an old gravel pit (in-filled with debris from the bombing of the City of London) on the Great South West Road was built over.

The cause of this building – the Underground – eventually had to be extended *under* this newly built-up area in the 1970s in order to reach Heathrow Airport, the only

open section being the crossing over the River Crane. Urbanisation of the Hounslow area was completed in less than a lifetime.

Work begins on the Central Line extensions. Plans to extend the Central London trains over the GWR's proposed Ealing & Shepherd's Bush Railway were put into operation after the first World War. The London County Council at this time began building its vast Wood Lane Estate west of White City and the new Tube extension was to include a wooden halt at East Acton to serve the estate. There was also a station at North Acton. The line was officially opened on 28 July 1920, with a lunch for the press and the Directors. The rapid growth of this part of London in the early 1920s resulted in a third station being opened – West Acton on 5 November 1923. The Central's terminus at Ealing Broadway was conveniently sited between that of the District and the GWR main-line station and all three stations were linked for easy passenger interchange.

The Central London quickly became popular with Ealing people as it provided a quicker, more direct route to the heart of the West End and the City than the District.

In 1936 a pair of separate tracks were provided for the GWR, to avoid increasing congestion. GWR local trains – often composed of saloon trailers and tank engines – also called at the three Acton stations, coming off the West London Railway. Work on the additional pair of lines was completed in 1938.

The LPTB New Works Plan provided for a long extension of the Central beside the GWR's High Wycombe line as far out as Denham. The GWR were to build the line, and Central Line trains would provide the through service from Essex, where a number of LNER suburban lines were to be electrified and worked by the Central.

Works began on the Central Line extensions in the late 1930s and by September 1939 were well advanced at least as far as

Greenford. Even beyond, bridges were being widened and sites cleared for stations. One of the earliest use of bulldozers was on the clearance of the vast site for the Ruislip Central Line Depot. Whilst the later buildings were completed by 1939, the increasing shortage of men and materials brought all works finally to a halt in about 1941. After the war, Greenford was opened in 1947 and West Ruislip in 1948. But the continuation to Denham was abandoned.

Suburban developments began along the line in the mid-1930s in anticipation of the Underground extensions. But the sites of the new stations and their GWR halt predecessors never attracted the shopping centres of the other lines. The districts near the line tended to be light industrial in nature. The houses were mainly of the terraced type seen in the Hounslow area. At Ruislip Gardens, and at South Ruislip, the edges of the vast Manor Homes Estate were within easy walking distance of the line. H. P. Taylor's Deane Park Estate got under way at South Ruislip (an area formerly known as Northolt Junction) by the late 1930s. Taylor's houses began along Victoria Road and Queen's Drive and Long Drive, but the estate was not finished until the 1950s. Some very early developments of small bungalows and chalets had taken place at South Ruislip almost from the opening of the GWR/GCR Joint line in the 1900s. But the area was never really built up with sufficient shops and amenities for many years.

At Denham, a parade of shops appeared and a few houses, but the proposed suburb was really just an appendage to the then famous Denham Film Studios.

The Surrey suburbs. The extension of the City & South London Tube to Morden was the only Underground line to penetrate into the Surrey suburbs in the 20th century. The network of lines inherited by the old Southern Railway had virtually created a monopoly of rail transport, except in the built-up old suburbs, where trams were important. Indeed, with the formation of the Southern Railway in 1923 and Sir Herbert Walker's impressive plans for the electrification, one finds it hard to justify the construction of any Tube line south of Clapham or the Elephant & Castle unless for a short section to capture traffic from the trams and buses of the inner suburbs.

But the Underground Group thought that there *was* ample scope. The Underground system was also attractive to many south Londoners, who admired the safe swift Underground of north London – smart and bright stations and trains so frequent that one didn't need a timetable; trains that took you direct to office or Oxford Street stores without a change; a system where the signs were easy to understand.

The City & South London Railway – the pioneer Tube line – was being modernised and its narrow-bore tunnels were converted to standard diameter at this time. A link was also constructed with the Hampstead Tube at Charing Cross so that eventually trains could run from either Highgate or Edgware southwards towards Morden via either the West End or the City. The section from Euston to Moorgate was closed from 9 August 1922 until 20 April 1924 for this work to be carried out. A further section was closed from Moorgate to Clapham Common from 29 November 1923 to 1 December 1924.

The plans for the southward extension to what was to be called 'North Morden' and a link from there with a proposed Wimbledon and Sutton railway were discussed in the early 1920s. But even Frank Pick and Lord Ashfield were no match for Sir Herbert Walker of the Southern. He was just as fanatical a publicist as they were and his 'Southern Electric' slogans and ever-expanding electrification schemes were impressive. He thought that the proposed extension of the Tube was a 'brutal intrusion into the area'.

So the Southern managed to get the scheme cut to 'North Morden' only and some years later the Wimbledon & Sutton

Railway, without the Underground link, was built by the Southern. However, even as late as 1944 there was talk at London Transport's Headquarters at 55 Broadway of eventually reaching North Cheam.

Work began on the City & South London extension to Morden (the 'North' was then dropped) on 31 December 1923. The line was in Tube tunnels to just north of Morden terminus, the area thus far having become built up by 1914. The line then continued south to the car sheds.

There were difficulties at Tooting Broadway where a subterranean reservoir was encountered. The severe winter of 1924–5 also delayed the works – particularly the clearing of the ground and the building of the car sheds at Morden.

During the latter part of 1925 and the beginning of 1926, the rolling stock was being delivered from the builders and had to be taken by road along narrow lanes to the depot.

The stations along the line were designed by Adams, Holden and Pearson and were specially built to stand out amid the 19th-century streets and shopping centres. They were best seen at night, where their floodlit facades were like beacons in the gloom of the south London suburbs – guiding lights that shone the way to the fast and clean trains that took you to the bright lights of the West End, or home to toast and tea beside the open fire of one of the new houses that spread all too quickly over the north Surrey fields.

The Morden extension was opened by Colonel J. T. Morre-Brabazon MP, the Parliamentary Secretary to the Minister of Transport. He drove the special train from Clapham South to Morden. There was the usual official lunch – held in the car sheds, where the tables were decorated with red and white carnations. Speakers at the lunch proposed high hopes for the line's future and possibly its extension. But Lord Ashfield emphasised that any further Tube extensions would have to create sufficient traffic to pay their way. To encourage travel

on the new line 15,000 free tickets were issued to people living near each station.

Morden terminus, very like Edgware in its design at track level, had a generous canopy over what was to be the pavement providing a bus station for the many routes that would connect far-flung places like Wallington, Cheam, Worcester Park, Mitcham, Banstead, Sutton and Esher.

At first, though, Morden stood alone in the flat fields, except for a couple of rows of old cottages and the 'Crown Inn'. On 31 July 1927, a large garage opened opposite the station, owned by an Underground subsidiary, Morden Station Garages Limited. Here one could park the car or cycle for the day and travel up to London on the Tube. The place was soon full and by the end of that year half-a-million people were using the trains each week at Morden alone. Overcrowding began to make life difficult for those living nearer London.

By the time the LCC's St Helier Estate was well under construction the Morden Line had become a by-word for overcrowding. St Helier was laid out on 825 acres of farm land south of Morden and was completed in 1934. The estate had its own shops and there were connecting bus routes to Morden, where long shopping parades soon grew along the country roads, to be joined by public houses and the inevitable cinema.

By the mid-1930s, travel on the Morden Line was becoming a daily horror for thousands. Matters came to a head in 1937, when passengers staged a series of sit-in strikes when they heard that their train was to be 'turned short' of its advertised destination. The Morden Line overcrowding became an issue in Parliament. The Minister of Transport, Dr Leslie Burg, urged London business firms to stagger their working hours. But little was done.

Sir Herbert Walker was not very pleased when he saw a drop in passenger traffic at his north Surrey stations. People still wanted the Tube. Despite all the discomforts, it did take them right to the centre of London instead of a vast and draughty terminus. It could also take them at weekends right to the new suburbs on the north side. 'From the hills of Middlesex to the hills of Surrey' was a publicity slogan of the time.

There were proposals for a relief tube line to be built from Kennington to Morden and Epsom, and one forward-looking estate developer in North Cheam advertised on a large board at the entrance to his estate, 'Coming this way,' with a picture of a Tube train.

But rising costs of materials in the late Thirties and the doubts that in the end the line would not pay its way, resulted in abandonment of the plans. The London and Home Counties Traffic Advisory Committee and a group of seven north Surrey councils urged more trains. But with the line's signalling system and the 'standard' type rolling stock, with its space-wasting motor cars, little could be done. One solution, which seems to have worked well, was the introduction of some 9-car trains, the first running on 8 November 1937. The platforms of some Edgware Line stations had to be lengthened. The idea was that the extra carriages only served certain stations on the journey in central London.

In 1938 the LPTB's Chief Mechanical Engineer, Dr W. S. Graff-Baker, introduced the first of a large number of new Tube trains, where the traction motors were placed beneath the floors, so increasing the passenger space. It was so successful that more cars of this type were manufactured than almost any other design of train in the world! The very last 1938 stock trains ran on the Bakerloo Line as late as 1985. For a time at least, the overcrowding became less of a problem. It was a case of the Morden Line being too much of a success!

North Ealing. A 1938 Tube stock train about to enter North Ealing station. North Ealing was to remain for many years one of the quietest stations on the west London Underground, as much of the area consisted of large Victorian property.

West London pastures. Looking over the valley towards Ealing from Horsenden Hill in 1919. The GWR Paddington-High Wycombe line and Perivale Halt are in the middle distance. Later the Central Line was to be extended along this route.

Sudbury Hill. Greenford Road looking north in the early 1920s, with the old District Line station on the left. The station was rebuilt in 1931–2 and parades of shops were built on the open ground behind the hedge.

Sudbury Town. Approach road to station, with open top bus. The old District Railway buildings were replaced by Holden's brick and concrete masterpiece of 1931.

STATION APPROACH, SUDBURY

Harrow. Watford Road near the junction with Sudbury Court Drive. The wide road, the builder's huts and new houses, and areas of adjacent countryside are typical of the 1930's. [Grange Museum]

Sudbury. Two views of the bus and tram terminus in the late 1920s.

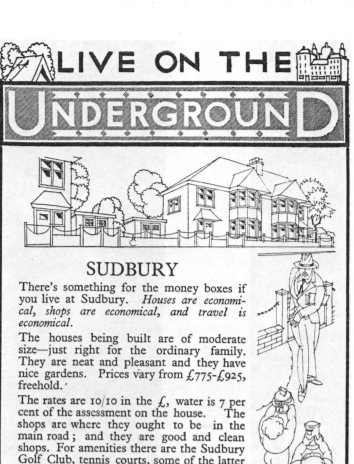

LIVE ON THE UNDERGROUND

SUDBURY

There's something for the money boxes if you live at Sudbury. *Houses are economical, shops are economical, and travel is economical.*

The houses being built are of moderate size—just right for the ordinary family. They are neat and pleasant and they have nice gardens. Prices vary from £775-£925, freehold.

The rates are 10/10 in the £, water is 7 per cent of the assessment on the house. The shops are where they ought to be in the main road; and they are good and clean shops. For amenities there are the Sudbury Golf Club, tennis courts, some of the latter atop of Horsendon Hill, with views over seven counties enabling the player to forsee the weather.

For train service, there is the Underground, which means that Sudbury enjoys cheap travel. A Season Ticket to Charing Cross costs 6/3 Weekly, 22/6 Monthly, 60/- Three monthly.

E1 13 27

Sudbury. An early Underground advertisement. This blended some hard-packed facts about the area with a fanciful drawing showing how the savings made by the average businessman could be placed immediately into the locked moneyboxes which his children would hold towards him upon his return home.

Sudbury Hill. A jolly scene imagined by the artist C. M. Jackson in 1933 to advertise the journey time and the season ticket prices to and from Sudbury Hill station. This was the image beloved of the time – men swopping flower cuttings, a housewife watching with respectful delight as her husband leaves with his golf-clubs on his back, whilst a happy child scooters up and down the new pavements as the sun casts long shadows from the lofty original parkland trees.

SUDBURY HILL

Journey Time	AND	Season Rates Weekly	Monthly
40 Mins.	CHARING CROSS	6/9	24/6
50 Mins.	MANSION HOUSE	7/3	26/6

C.M. JACKSON

Perivale. Perivale station, Great Western Railway, later to be served by the Central Line. This scene, taken in 1935, shows a bill board for Cliffords Houses at £595 on their so-called Perivale Park Estate. This was the average 'going' price for terraced houses during the 1930s in the London suburban area. The station itself, really just a halt, is strutted with timber sleepers, and boasts only a series of small station huts to protect the new house owners from the elements.

Northolt. Mid-1930s: Clifford Homes arise out of the mist beyond the railway. One terraced block is roofed, another stands ready, whilst beyond are the foundations for further homes. Although some work was carried out, the Central Line did not open until 1948.

Uxbridge. 'Standard' type Piccadilly train arriving at Belmont Road in 1933. The 'through' running from South Harrow began on 23 October of that year.

Ealing. A 6-car train on the Central Line on the section from Shepherd's Bush to Ealing in the early 1920s.

Alperton. When the station opened in 1903, it was called Perivale-Alperton and in 1910 was renamed Alperton for Perivale and Wembley. The cottages seen through the bridge were later demolished to make way for a bus garage in LPTB days and the station was rebuilt in 1931. It is one of the few Underground stations where escalators take passengers *up* to the trains.

South Harrow. Two 'ST' buses, still with the fleet-name 'General', wait outside the old District Line station and building. The new LPTB has already put the words 'London Transport' over the timetables on the right. The new station was opened more conveniently by the Northolt Road bridge and the shops in 1935, but the original building shown here still exists.

South Harrow. This picture was taken not long after the station opened on 28 June 1903. The platforms are wooden and the sign reads 'South Harrow for Roxeth and Northolt'.

The Uxbridge Road. Trolleybus in the Uxbridge Road on 19 August 1960, a few months before being replaced by buses. The trolleybuses and the trams provided useful feeder services to the Ealing Underground stations from places as far away as Hayes.

Give them a better outlook in 1933!

Your rent will buy them a home at Greenford; give them greater happiness—better health—and a heritage which You can enjoy for a lifetime. We make this great step simple—you make the Future secure.

FOR £10 CASH YOU MOVE IN

Your Building Society Repayments, INCLUSIVE of all Road Charges, Legal Fees, etc, are from

16/6 WEEKLY—*NO EXTRAS*

Greenford Homes are 2 minutes walk from Sudbury Hill Station. 354 trains daily carry you to and from the City and West End without any change, or bus or tram ride. Season Ticket (to Piccadilly or Temple Station) 5/7 weekly). Run out this week-end and inspect these full-value houses, built to last for generations. All are FREEHOLD.
ACCOMMODATION: 3 Bedrooms, 2 Living Rooms, Tiled Bathroom and fully fitted light-labour Kitchen. Every house completely decorated and ready for occupation.
Post the Coupon below for Plans, and Details of the simple Costain-Owner-Purchaser Plan—founded upon 60 years of home-building experience.

COUPON.

To Richard Costain & Sons, Ltd.,
    Estate Office, Greenford Road,
        Greenford, Middlesex.
Please send plans and copy of your book without obligation to

Name ....

Address ....

....

BLOCK LETTERS PLEASE   E.F.

Sudbury Hill. Typical estate agent's advertisement. This one is for houses along Whitton Avenue and district. But they were certainly more than the two minutes' walk from the station mentioned in the copy!

Boston Manor. The station building shown here dated from 1883 and was similar to that at Osterley and Spring Grove. Rebuilding of Boston Manor took place in 1934. At Boston Manor, Holden designed a tower above the new building that echoed the contemporary style he had seen in the Netherlands.

The tram tracks in front of the old station were for route 55 which ran the short distance from Brentford Half Acre to Hanwell (extended to Acton in rush hours).

District Railway 'M' class trailer. One of a number of new cars built in 1933 to replace some of the ageing original fleet.

Ealing Broadway station. The District station opened in 1879, a few hundred yards from the GWR main-line station, and had an impressive villa-like station building facing a (then) tree-less Haven Green.

Ealing. A popular Saturday shopping centre in the inter-war years. The inhabitants of the newer suburbs would come in by bus and train to shop and have tea at Elred Sayers or John Saunders (the shops behind the bus).

Northfields. Looking north along Northfields Avenue about 80 years ago. When the District Line was electrified to Hounslow, suburban development was rapid. The station opened in 1908 as Northfield [no s!] (Ealing). In 1911 it was renamed Northfields and Little Ealing. After the rebuilding of 1932, the second name was dropped. The station was designed by Stanley Heaps. The Northfields train depot (with a capacity for 304 cars) was completed in 1932. With the arrival of the Piccadilly trains, houses spread across the remaining land. The shopping parades were graced by Cecil Maset's flamboyant Spanish-style cinema of 1932 (known as the Spanish City). Not far from the station stood Niagara House, the home of the French rope-walker Charles Blondin, who crossed the Niagara Falls several times on his rope. The house was demolished in 1935 and Blondin Avenue stands on the site.

Northfields and Little Ealing station. This view of the old station platforms, taken in 1920, gives a good idea of what District Line surface stations were like before modernisation. The view has changed little when compared with platforms at Boston Manor today, although the large iron signs, which could be seen screwed to any available point, have long been swept away. This station opened in 1908.

South Ealing. District 'F' class train with passenger about to board, using the hand-operated doors. These trains were built by the Metropolitan Carriage and Wagon Finance Co. The company had been building war tanks and it is said that the 'F' class trains got their nickname 'The Tanks' because of this. They ran, with some modernisation, until the early 1960s on the Metropolitan.

A pair of extra tracks were laid down from Acton Town to Northfields in readiness for the Piccadilly Line extension in 1932, and South Ealing was rebuilt as a two-island platform station, but with a temporary booking hall. The temporary accommodation is still in use!

Uxbridge. The remains of the old station about 1965. It was superseded by Holden's High Street terminus in December 1938. The new building was similar to Cockfosters.

District Line Poster. Light, power and speed – the magic trinity of words that, in 1910, were supposed to convey, in a short phrase, all the exciting advantages of the new District Railway's electric trains. The poster was by C. Sharland.

Isleworth. London Road, Isleworth, at Busch Corner about 1909. The open-top tramcar linked Brentford with Hounslow (turning at 'Bell' corner). These trams were replaced by trolleybuses in 1935. It is interesting to note that fixed stopping points, marked with flags, existed so far out in this semi-rural environment.

Hounslow East. Hounslow Town station, when a building was finally placed on the direct line with Hounslow Barracks station. Hounslow Town station was originally sited closer to the town, on a loop line.

Hounslow West. A 'B' type bus (1425) waits at Hounslow Barracks station, District Railway in 1921. Bus route 82 ran between the station and Staines, serving the areas of Bedfont and Feltham Cross, later to be styled 'Hounslow Garden Suburb'. The route later became identified with bus route 116 from Hounslow bus garage, running to Egham.

Hounslow Central. Hounslow had a third station known as Heston Hounslow, with buildings that were little more than a tin shed. It was to become Hounslow Central station, and a focus for builders' cars which met London trains so that potential customers could be hurried off to see the new estates at Bedfont, Feltham, and Cranford in the 1930s.

Things were rather different during the days when Hounslow trains were hauled by District Railway steam locomotives, as one driver, Mr Membery, recalled upon his retirement in 1929: 'The Hounslow trains used to run empty. There was simply no traffic on the line, and the builders who started putting up new houses on 'spec' got it in the neck properly. Things were so bad that they had to allow people to live in 'em rent free, so that the property shouldn't go to rot. A lot of the District Railway men got nice little houses in this way. To my mind, the District Railway didn't set itself out to buck up the Hounslow traffic. They ought to have taken a hint from what the old GER were doing for Walthamstow by running trains at low fares. It'd have paid 'em in the end. Going to Hounslow was about as lively a trip for traffic as the old LSWR service between Turnham Green and Shepherd's Bush.'

Hounslow. Hounslow High Street at the Broadway, April 1937. The trams have gone, and the new route 657 trolleybuses sweep people away towards Brentford. There is an air of stagnation as the High Street adapts itself to its role as a service area for the new estates of Hanworth, Hounslow West and Cranford. This part of Hounslow High Street was not so popular with shoppers as the 'Bell' area, at the western end.

Hounslow. Hounslow High Street, at Broadway Corner, looking west towards the 'Bell', about 1908. Very little traffic competes with the tram, and a mounted policeman has a quiet time. Although the coming of the District Railway had linked Hounslow with London, it had not caused the change that was to occur with the arrival of the Piccadilly Line extension to Hounslow some decades later.

Cranford. Cranford, even in the early 1930s, was just an unspoilt village that had not made up its mind between remaining around the mansion of the Berkeley family (Cranford House) or of sitting astride the Bath Road. This view shows the Bath Road at Cranford. The bridge over the river Crane is recent, but the main road is still surfaced by dripping a light coating of tar upon it and covering with light shingle thrown at random from a horse-drawn contractor's wagon. There is no proper kerb-line, and in this 1920s photograph, only the pub, and Leake the bakers, line the north side of the carriageway. Further eastward came the orchard of the 'Berkeley Arms', a pub which was to be aggrandised into a hostelry, sporting French chateau-type architecture and towers.

Leake's were to remain as bakers serving Cranford into the 1950s. They had a justifiable reputation for their home-baked bread and cakes at a time when new multiple bakeries were starting to flourish.

There is every reason to think of Harris-built Houses as Happy Homes. The houses are well built. The rooms are of ample proportions for displaying your furniture to the best advantage.

The careful planning and equipment of the tiled kitchenette meet all the requirements of the modern home, thus reducing the household duties in this department to an absolute minimum.

The Bedroom

Cranford. W. Harris was one of the major builders in the Hounslow area during the 1930s. From the spacious estate office at Hounslow West, opposite the station, he superintended developments in the Heston and Cranford areas, then orchard land. Every effort was made to please customers, and Harris issued a multi-page booklet to induce waverers to plump for a Harris-built home. The illustration shows a page from this rare publication.

Cranford: Great South West Road. The river Crane and the Great South-West Road bridge, photographed by the authors in 1943. The area on the right of the river was rich orchard land, and was to be overbuilt with the huge hangars of Heathrow maintenance section just after the war. The Piccadilly Line extension to Heathrow now passes over the Crane just forward of the bridge. Note the concrete anti-tank barriers on the bridge approach, set up during the 1940 invasion scare.

Cranford. Cranford Lane, about 1929. A lost arcadia, indeed! A real lane at this time, winding amid shady trees watered from a gentle wayside stream (long gone), Cranford Lane was soon to be straightened and lined by houses. Nearby was Heston Airport, where Chamberlain had landed after seeing Herr Hitler; it was foreseen that the airfield would develop steadily to link Hounslow with countries beyond the seas. This dream was to be eclipsed with the grandiose Heathrow Airport scheme just after the second World War.

Oval. South London's Tube station in May 1927. The placard reads
'Trunk: amazing new theory' – a reference to the Trunk murder that was
the talk of Town at the time. This was a busy intersection and after the
second World War was to be a notorious bottleneck. The large display
map outside the station was the predecessor of the useful '¼ mile radius'
maps of later years, to be found in all Underground vestibules and
booking halls. Oval was one of several new station reconstructions in
1924, faced with cream-coloured terracotta with black dressings.

Clapham Common. A wartime summer scene on the South London Railway's Clapham Common station in 1915. In spite of the lack of station identity, an announcement of the Company's earlier extension from the Angel to King's Cross and Euston is displayed, in paint, around the entire cornice of the building in Clapham Park Road.

Clapham South. The original City & South London Tube was opened on 4 November 1890 by King Edward VII, then Prince of Wales. On 1 December 1924 the reconstructed Tube, with tunnel widening and re-equipping, was reinaugurated at Clapham Common station with great publicity: 'The small kiosk-like structure that serves as entrance from the corner of the Common and the staircase enclosure that gives entrance . . . afford little indication of the extensiveness of the works that have been carried out below ground,' said the *Clapham Observer*. Quickly, the line was linked northwards with the extension to Edgware; also at that time it was announced that a 5-mile extension was already in hand for a line between Clapham and Morden projecting the railway to the 'rural environs of London on the Epsom Road'. The first of these new stations that was to form the Morden extension was at Nightingale Lane, seen in this photograph taken in August, 1924. The station was later called 'Clapham South'.

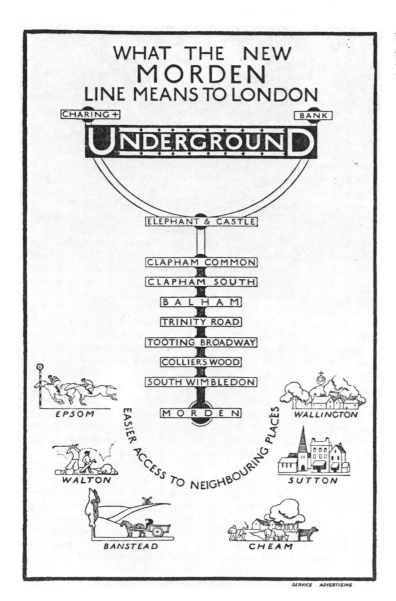

Underground press advertising. An attempt to show that unsavoured country delights lay in store for Londoners when the new extension to Morden was

Morden. In August 1924, when this picture was taken, the ground for the new terminus at Morden was already earmarked, and appropriate signs erected. It was, of course, completely rural, laced by the occasional fieldpath. Bus loads of sightseers can be seen peering over the lost land from the open top of the vehicle.

Morden. The development of Morden: This scene shows Morden station and its forecourt shortly after the main station building was erected. Hoardings on each side cover the ancillary shop development. The ancient trees still manage to survive, and only one bus is needed, for the great housing estates are yet to arise. The *South London Press* had predicted in 1925: 'The extension to Edgware has already inspired the laying-out of estates on garden suburb lines in that remote town, or rather village, and also around the new station at Hendon. Similar activity can be looked for at Morden. Indeed, schemes of development are already in course of promotion.' Minds of the time were untroubled at the thought of swamping rural land with seas of brick and mortar; indeed, the open countryside lured the planners into great efforts of railway extension, causing the rapid spread of urbanisation within a decade or so.

Morden. Work on the Morden extension. The Morden extension lines came to the surface just before the approach to the terminus.

A steam shovel of the type that had changed very little since the turn of the century is at work in completely open countryside just north of Morden station in October 1925. The ground is being excavated prior to track-laying, and the concrete retaining walls have already been erected.

The

Cab
1926
of b

Morden station grows up
The station in June 1927, with the shops built and about to open for
trade. A 165 bus waits to run to Banstead, but still there are more cycles
than cars.

Morden rush hour. The scene during the early morning rush hour in
April 1938. A long ticket queue has already formed as people hurry off
the 164 and 156 buses on their journeys to London. An 80 bus waits to go
to Walton-on-the-Hill, one of London Transport's longest surviving
central bus routes.

Morden station forecourt, with 'NS' and 'STL' buses. The forecourt was filled with special Epsom race excursion buses during Derby week, a practice that reached its zenith during the late 1930s.

Morden. A experimental unit of nine cars at Morden sidings. Note the Morden-Edgware Line markings carried by the motor car.

LONDON PASSENGER TRANSPORT BOARD
MAP OF NEW WORKS PROGRAMME, 1935–1940

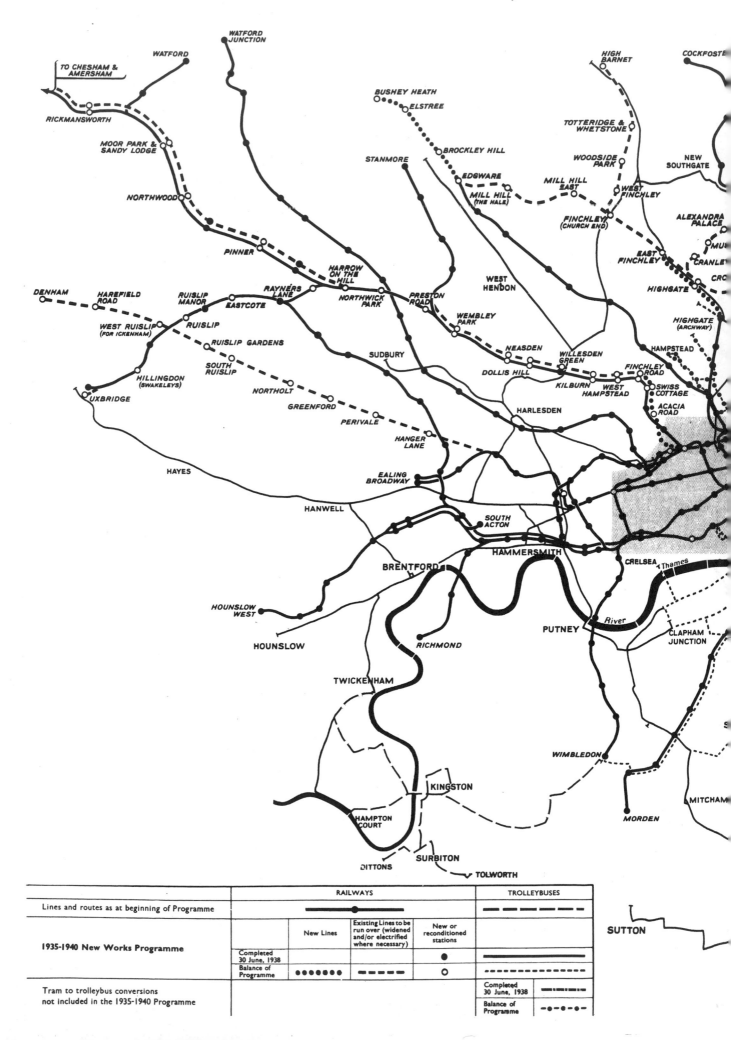

		RAILWAYS			TROLLEYBUSES	
Lines and routes as at beginning of Programme						
1935-1940 New Works Programme		New Lines	Existing Lines to be run over (widened and/or electrified where necessary)	New or reconditioned stations		
	Completed 30 June, 1938			●		
	Balance of Programme	●●●●●●●	– – – – –	○		
Tram to trolleybus conversions not included in the 1935-1940 Programme					Completed 30 June, 1938	
					Balance of Programme	